A Japanese Artist in London

Yoshio Markino

introduced by
Sammy I Tsunematsu

In Print
1991

First published in 1910.

First published in this edition in 1991 by In Print Publishing Ltd, 9 Beaufort Terrace, Brighton BN2 2SU, UK.

Introduction © 1991 Sammy I. Tsunematsu

In Print Publishing Ltd is registered with the Publishers Licensing Society in the UK and the Copyright Clearance Center in the USA.

British Library Cataloguing in Publication Data: A catalogue record for this book is available from the British Library.

ISBN 1 873047 00 2

Cover illustration – *Autumn* by Yoshio Markino
Cover design by Russell Townsend
Introduction typeset by MC Typeset Ltd
Printed and bound by Utopia Press

Contents

Illustrations . . . . [iv]
Introduction . . . . [v]
Acknowledgements . . . . [xxvi]

A Japanese Artist in London

Appreciation vii
Preface xiii

I	My arrival in England	1
II	My life in Greenwich	13
III	My life in New Cross	20
IV	My life in Kensal Rise	36
V	At the tombstone-maker's in Norwood	48
VI	My life in Brixton	57
VII	I decide to commit suicide	70
VIII	The loosening of the rope	76
IX	'The Darling of the Gods'	96
X	I become a Chelsea conservative	102
XI	Some Japanese impressions of England	117
XII	My Japanese friends	136
XIII	'The Colour of London'	146
XIV	In the West London Hospital – before the operation	151
XV	In the West London Hospital – after the operation	162
XVI	My holidays in London	178
XVII	Concluding chapter	188

Illustrations

Colour

Constitution Arch
Autumn
Regent's Park
Life class
Earl's Court Station★
Outside St George's Hospital★
Hyde Park Corner★
The Thames at Ranelagh★

Black and white

Tombstone designed by Markino
Flower sales girl
Home of the Chelsea Conservative:
  68 Sydney Street
Markino's friend Hara *and* Markino
  in hospital

★Reproduced from the original edition.

INTRODUCTION

Yoshio Markino – the painter of fog

In the autumn of 1976, I went into a second-hand bookshop in front of the British Museum and looked along the shelves. I was not searching for any particular book. There was just a vague feeling that there might be a new magazine that had been published at the time when Soseki Natsume[1] was studying in London. But there I was to come across the book which would change my life. The book was on the left-hand side of the bottom shelf of the bookcase, covered with dust. It was a place not seen unless you made a point of stooping down. The book I chanced to hold in my hand was strange, with the title written in Japanese on a blue cover, *Nihonjin Gako – London Nikki*. The author's name, Yoshio Markino, was written in English. Yoshio was without a doubt a Japanese name, but what nationality was the writer? On closer inspection, I read Yoshio Makino (written in Japanese).[2] It had to be an anglicized Japanese name. The book was published in 1910, which meant that the

---

[1] Soseki Natsume is the pseudonym of Kin'nosuke Natsume (born 5 January 1867, Tokyo; died 9 December 1916, Tokyo). Soseki's novels include *I am a Cat* (1905), *Botchan* (1906) and *Kokoro* (1914). As with other Japanese names in this introduction, I have adopted Western word order for Soseki's name, although, confusingly, even Japanese people refer to him by his first name pseudonym, Soseki.

[2] The correct romanization of the author's name is Makino. However, he added the 'r' to assist non-Japanese in the pronunciation. As the spelling is Markino throughout the first edition of *A Japanese Artist in London*, this is the form I have used.

INTRODUCTION

writer must have been living in London for some time before that. Perhaps at the same time as Soseki? At the beginning of the book there was a tribute by Douglas Sladen, and on reading the preface, I came across the name, Wakamiya, a Japanese friend. Whoever was Wakamiya? Continuing to read absorbedly, I was excited to find other Japanese names such as Hara, Hidaka, Morinami. Reading on eagerly with the thought that perhaps Soseki Natsume's name would appear, I had soon finished 60 pages. When I chanced to look behind me, the bald shopkeeper said 'I'm closing'. Then, pointing to the book I was holding, he explained, 'Markino was probably the most famous Japanese in the United Kingdom. He painted beautiful watercolours of the famous sights of London. Not only that, but he was also an essayist who wrote many books in English'.

At that time I was living in some poverty, so holding up the Markino autobiography I had in my hand, I said 'Look at this! It is covered in dust. Can't you knock something off because of its filthy state . . . ?' The shopkeeper replied, 'Sir, the dust is part of its value'. While being taken aback by this unexpected reply, at the same time I felt ashamed of myself for having dreamt of haggling over the book in which Markino recounts the trials which drove him to consider suicide. I bought the book on the spot. I was so excited that I do not remember the price. Wanting to finish it as quickly as possible, I carried on reading with a beer in one hand at a pub four or five buildings along from the bookshop. The more I read, the more clearly I understood Markino's troubles, and my curiosity was aroused.

Publication of A Japanese Artist in London

In mid-December 1909, having completed the illustrations for *Oxford from Within* (published 1910) Markino

INTRODUCTION

returned to a hotel above South Kensington station. After Christmas, he paid a New Year call on Mr Spielmann, Editor of the art journal *Magazine of Art*. On that occasion, Spielmann told him 'I have spoken to the publisher, Chatto & Windus, about publishing your illustrated autobiography, so please write a manuscript immediately. The fee will be £25 initially and £50 if it is successful', he was told. When he heard this Douglas Sladen, a friend who had taken on the responsibility of Markino's literary agent, declared '£25, or even £50, is too little. You should expect a fee of over £1,000. I'll negotiate with Chatto & Windus'. So Markino visited Mr Spalding, the Chairman, at Chatto & Windus with Sladen. When Sladen demanded royalties of 15% on the first 2,000 books sold, 20% for up to 5,000 copies and 25% for over 5,000, Spalding laughingly declared, 'I do not for a minute dream that the book will sell over 5,000 copies, but a contract's a contract and we'll agree on that'. He had his secretary type it up immediately. Thanks to this, Markino's autobiography, *A Japanese Artist in London*, which sold as well as Sladen had predicted, exceeded £1,000 in royalties in just under six months. Markino bathed in the praises of the newspapers of the day: 'Mr Markino's book is literature by virtue of its artlessness: he plies the jaded literary appetite with a new dish' (*The Times*); 'Mr Markino's book has a deep human interest, because it is so frank, so simple, so quaintly original . . . The whole book is full of quaint and characteristic observations' (*Daily Telegraph*); and, 'Seldom have we read anything with more delight and amusement. Mr Markino's English is inimitable: he has forged out of a foreign language a medium of his own which really reflects his mind and expresses his feelings with wonderful terseness' (*World*). Contemporary society buzzed with talk of Markino and he became a favourite of the period.

INTRODUCTION

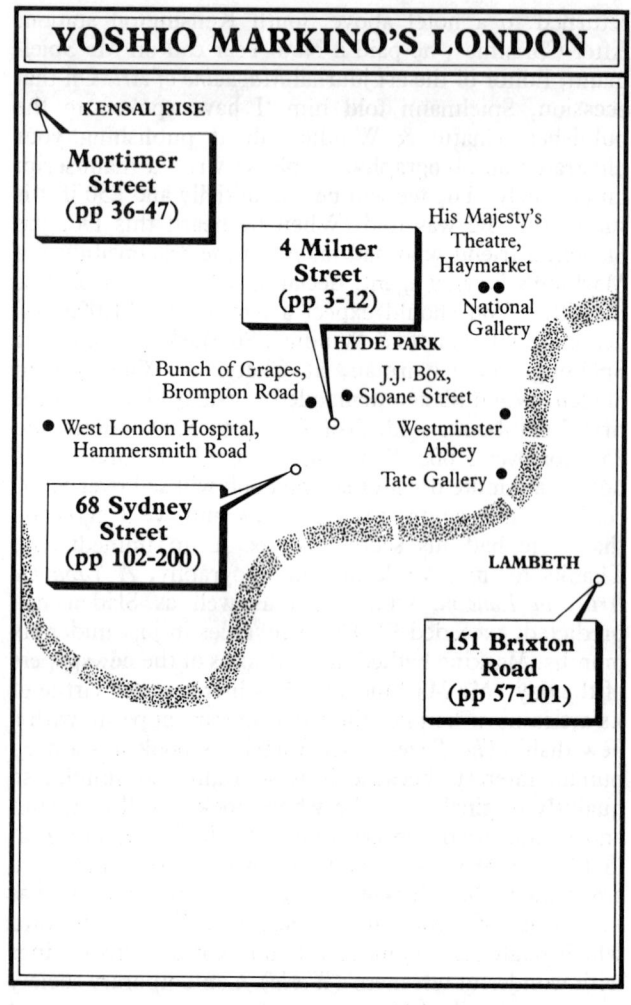

INTRODUCTION

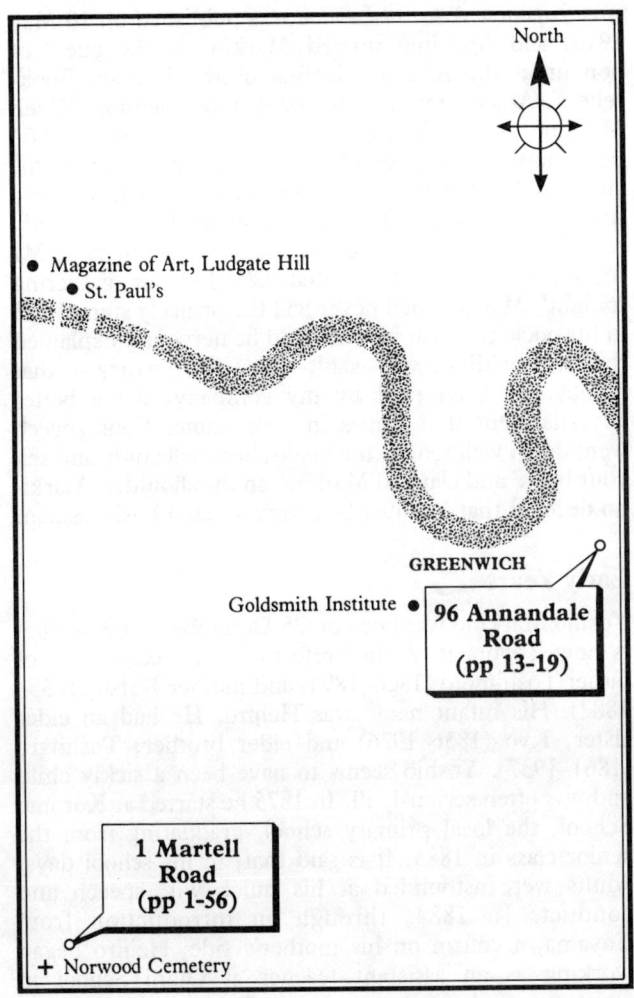

INTRODUCTION

A Japanese Artist in London was published on 10 May 1910, and Spalding invited Markino to be guest of honour at the Annual Meeting of the London Booksellers' Association on the preceding evening. When Markino arrived at the venue, there were nearly 500 bookshop owners present, and, as usual, he made his audience laugh with a humorous speech. When Markino finished speaking, for some reason Spalding suddenly rose to the dais and said: 'Ladies and Gentlemen, Mr Markino has kindly donated £25 for our gathering tonight'. Markino had never had the princely sum of £25 in his pocket, and at his wit's end he nervously explained this to Spalding, who said, 'Oh, don't worry – that money has been paid by my company, it's a better advertisement if it comes in your name. Your speech went down well too, so the booksellers will study and sell your book' and clapped Markino on the shoulder. Markino decided that he must be a very shrewd businessman.

Early Years

Yoshio Markino was born on 25 December 1869 in what is now Toyota in Aichi Prefecture, the second son of father Toshimoto (1826–1894) and mother Katsu (1835–1882). His infant name was Heijiro. He had an elder sister, Kyo (1856–1926) and elder brother, Toshitaro (1861–1937). Yoshio seems to have been a sickly child and was often seriously ill. In 1875 he started at Koromo School, the local primary school, graduating from the senior class in 1883. It is said that, in his school days, adults were astounded at his quick wit, speech and conduct. In 1884, through an introduction from Toyama, a cousin on his mother's side, Heijiro began working as an assistant teacher at Otani School in Chita-gun and, again thanks to Toyama, was shortly afterwards adopted into the Isogai family from a nearby

INTRODUCTION

village. However, because there was already a Heijiro in that family, his name was changed to Yoshio to avoid confusion. Yoshio remained fond of his infant name, Heijiro, all his life and, in London, when inscribing copies of his books as presents, he often signed his name Heiji or Heijiro Markino.

In 1886 he became assistant teacher at the primary school at which his brother, Toshitaro, worked. He lived with his brother and, on Wednesdays and Saturdays, made the walk of several hours to attend school in Nagoya. He learned Western style sketching from Kanekiyo Nozaki (1862–1936) and Manji Mizuno (1863–1911). At about that time he met an American Missionary, Klein, and began to study under him, living at the church and devoting himself to the study of English. At that time he was very impressed by Washington Irving's *Sketchbook* and, fascinated by the scenery and lives of the people depicted there, began to dream of travelling to America or Britain to study English literature. Klein established the Nagoya Eiwa School (present-day Nagoya Gakuin) in 1887, and Yoshio was baptised there. In October 1892, immediately after graduating from Nagoya Eiwa School, Markino borrowed money for the journey from his sister and went to Yokohama to stay with Maki Hotta, a cousin on his father's side. There he waited for an opportunity to travel overseas. Through an introduction from his cousin, Goto, he soon got to know the famous watercolour artist, Shigetaka Shiga who gave him a letter of introduction to the then Consul in San Francisco, Sutemi Chinda. With this, his long-held dream of going to America was realized.

Yokohama to San Francisco

At ten o'clock on 29 June 1893, the British P&O steam ship *Peru* began to board. Markino rose at nine o'clock

INTRODUCTION

and, with his aunt, Maki and friend Shotaro Kawanishi, left his lodgings to go to the quayside. At that time, Yokohama port was still under construction and there were as yet no boarding bridges, so Markino made his way to the *Peru* in a small boat. There was great confusion on the *Peru* as the luggage which had come by lighter was brought aboard. The *Peru* was a 4,000 ton wooden ship, and the smallest on the San Francisco–Hong Kong run, but to Markino, who had only ever seen Japanese ships, it seemed enormous. This impression was mingled with feelings of admiration and unease towards that great country, America, which he had never seen. On the deck at half past eleven, the departure bell began to boom. Those who had come to see off passengers began to run. On parting, the tearful Maki told him, 'Heiji, you are honest and I trust you implicitly. You have always done as I said, so I feel very responsible for you. Listen to me, Heiji. What is so dear to me is not your body, but your beautiful spirit. If you begin to miss me and come home with your studies half finished, I will not even turn to look at you. It doesn't matter how long it takes, just study to the very end, and develop to the full the talent given to you by God. Do you understand?' 'Mmm', Markino just nodded in agreement. Turning to the aunt and Kawanishi standing behind her, Maki apologized, 'Excuse me', and, kissing Markino lightly, continued, 'Heiji, this is a sacred oath made before heaven'. As their lighter began to row away from *Peru*, the three of them stood up and waved their handkerchiefs. On deck, Markino replied with his, until he could no longer distinguish faces or hands in the lighter. At exactly twelve noon, the siren sounded loudly, and to Heiji it was as though the sound pierced him through. The ship turned almost 90 degrees causing the sea to boil into a pure white eddy. To Markino it seemed as though even this eddy was giving its blessing to his future. The

INTRODUCTION

day he had waited and waited for for fourteen years since the age of seven had finally come.

There were 13 Japanese passengers on the *Peru*. He got to know Sen Tsuda (father of Umeko Tsuda, the founder of Tsuda Women's University in Tokyo), a first class passenger on his way to Chicago for the World Exposition, and in the third class, Masui, a San Francisco laundryman, who was aiming to study engineering at Tokyo University and was travelling to America to earn the school fees. Due to his ability to speak English, Markino also became friendly with crew members. It was very lively on board, with a party held on 4 July to celebrate American Independence Day. They entered port at Honolulu on the evening of 8 July, and went ashore the following morning. Masui took Markino to a Japanese public bath, and, feeling refreshed for the first time in many days, they went to a Japanese restaurant run by a friend of Masui. Leaving Honolulu at five o'clock, the *Peru* set off once again across the Pacific, on course for America. They met with adverse winds and suffered from rough seas on the way over, but arrived at San Francisco on the evening of 18 July. The following morning, Markino finally stepped on to the land he admired so much.

The Decision to Study Painting

Waiting for him on his arrival in San Francisco, Markino found Utsujiro Suzuki, who came from the same village and had been alerted by the alumnus of Koromo School. He was seven years older than Markino and a pupil of his father Toshimoto: it was the first time they had met in ten years. After graduating from the Theology Department of Meiji Gakuin University, he had worked as a priest doing evangelical work in Fukui Prefecture. In recognition of his services, he had received permission to

INTRODUCTION

study in America for three years and had arrived two or three months previously. He was studying at Berkeley, but, being on summer vacation until 15 September, undertook to show Markino around.

Under Utsujiro's leadership they immediately set out to see the city. Along Montgomery Street, the splendid buildings of the banks, insurance companies and shipping companies, the beauty of the store fittings, and the orderly streets, were a revelation to him. On Kearnay Street they saw a Japanese store called Kai Shoten decorated with Japanese gold screens and bright kimono and with Gifu lanterns suspended from the ceiling. After walking some more they came to a splendid wooden building. Utsujiro explained that this was Hopkins Art School. Mark Hopkins, a millionaire who had come from the east during the upheaval of the Gold Rush 60 or 70 years earlier, and struck gold, bequeathed his home to the university at Berkeley. His home, which faced on to California Street became an art gallery, and the building on Pine Street the Art School. Markino had come to America to study English literature, and, while enjoying drawing, little dreamt that he would one day study at the Hopkins Art School.

That night he stayed at Utsujiro's lodgings, the YMCA on 201 Heyt Street, and immediately wrote to the people who had been so kind to him. First he made two copies of a journal of his voyage which came to over ten densely covered pages of small writing, to which he added an account of his impressions of the sights he had seen since coming ashore. He sent one letter to Maki Hotta, one to his family in Koromo and one to Hideko Mano in Nagoya. The next morning, Markino went with Utsujiro to the Japanese Consulate in Pine Street to present Shigetaka Shiga's letter of introduction to the Consul, Sutemi Chinda and to discuss his future. On hearing Markino's aims in coming to America, Chinda explained

INTRODUCTION

the difficulties for a Japanese studying English literature and put to him the advantages of painting. Heeding Chinda's warning that 'it is not possible for foreigners to become authorities on literature', Markino resolved to concentrate on the study of art and to continue with literature as an interest.

In the two months before 15 September, the new term at Hopkins Art School, which he had chosen on Chinda's recommendation, he decided to do housework to earn money for school fees. Until finding work he visited the sights with Utsujiro, and called on Terutake Hinata of the Japan–US Trading Company on Powell Street, Masao Yamato, President of the San Francisco Newspaper on O'Farrell Street, and Hajime Nagai, President of the Kinmon Shinposha on Stevenson Street to learn about the area. On another day, Utsujiro took him to Cliff House in the suburbs. The crashing white waves at the bottom of the cliffs facing the Pacific were an amazing sight. He made 20 or 30 sketches of the Pacific, the rocky cliffs, white waves, and fur seals. They also went to see the nearby Baker Beach. The coastal scenery by these cliffs was incredible. Later, while studying at the Art School, Markino often came here to paint watercolours and oil paintings. An oil painting which seems to be from this period still remains in the Markino family. On the lid of a Havana cigar box is a painting of a scene which appears to be Baker Beach and in black ink on the reverse he has written, 'Near San Francisco, North America, Yoshio Markino 1897'.

The Struggle for School Fees

Having decided to enter Hopkins Art School on Chinda's recommendation, Markino asked Inazawa, Director of the YMCA, to help him find a job as School Boy in order to earn as much of the fees as possible before school

INTRODUCTION

started. At that time there was no work for Japanese in America except dishwashing and housework. The weekly rate for eight hours a day of housework was $3.50. The rate for a School Boy, who was allowed to attend school during the day and worked for one and a half hours in the morning and two and a half hours in the evening, was $1.50. Markino's first employer on an introduction from Inazawa was a family of Hungarian immigrants. The husband and wife were 54 and 55, and, with two boys of about 30 and a 17 year old daughter, they were a family of five. They had come to America about 20 years previously. At that time, many Japanese immigrants were going to Hawaii and these soon made their way to San Francisco. The numbers of rough-mannered Japanese, who were only working for the money, increased. For this reason, the bourgeoisie would not employ Japanese, and, because the Japanese would work for low wages, the families who did employ them were poor.

In the Hungarian family to which Markino first went, the housewife announced in halting English, 'Jap names are difficult, so I have called all the other Japs I've had here, George. I shall call you George too, so don't forget'. George was made to work for 14 solid hours a day, from five in the morning until eight at night, helping with the three meals and cleaning the house and garden. The daughter, Maria, was in the third grade of Presidio Girls' High School, loved art, and was hoping to go to Hopkins Art School. She called him Heiji and they got on well together. Moreover, the friendship of the female students he got to know through her made his later stay in America very enjoyable. However, the work in that household was very strenuous, and realising he would have no time to study there, Markino left after three weeks.

On the ninth or tenth day in his next job, a family of

INTRODUCTION

two girls and an old lady at 18 Geary Street, Markino slipped and fell when carrying the dishes from the old lady's meal downstairs. A sharp can opener cut him from the tip of his left thumb to his wrist injuring him seriously. The elder girl, who had been a nurse, applied first aid and called a doctor. However, he was no longer able to work. The younger girl's fiancé felt sorry for him and gave him $25 to help out with his living expenses. Markino had no alternative but to return to the YMCA. While he was still recovering there, 15 September and the new term came and went. Markino had the $25, but after paying for his lodgings, there was not enough to start school. Luckily, unlike other universities, it was possible to start at the Art School mid term, so he decided to work for a further five or six weeks. This time he travelled by boat to Oakland and then to Bolleo, a small village one hour to the east by train, to the Fisher family. The wages were good, $4 a week, so in six weeks he was able to save $24.

Hopkins Art School

On the morning of 3 November, Markino went to Hopkins Art School and at last completed the registration procedures. Umataro Ide, who was later to help him find lodgings in Annandale Road, London and Kiyoshi Natsui, from Keio University, had just completed their studies here. Natsui soon returned to Japan, while Ide went to Europe and worked in hotels to earn his fees. Mango Kobayashi (1871–1911) was studying at the time. His real name was Hanakichi Kobayashi and he later exhibited work at the Hakubakai, but he used the pseudonym Mango all his life. In his autobiography *Asaki Yume Mishi (Idle Dreams)*, Markino wrote of Hanakichi Kobayashi: 'Mango Kobayashi was still attending school, but he was already streets ahead of me

INTRODUCTION

in painting nudes in oil'. Katsuzo Takahashi returned to Japan just as Markino was beginning his studies, and exhibited approximately 20 of his American works in the 6th Meiji Art Exhibition (1894), where they made quite a stir. He had studied at the forerunner of Hopkins, the San Francisco School of Design. It is said that the watercolourist, Katsumi Miyake (1874–1954), saw Takahashi's watercolours and resolved to go to America.

The Head of the School when Markino started was Arthur Matthew, a man of about 35 or 36 who had studied in Paris under Boulanger. He came to the school to teach three times a week. A Frenchman, Duran, of about 30, was assistant professor; portrait painting was taught by a German, Kuhnas; and landscape painting by Yelland, in his forties. Alabaster sculptures of the gods of ancient Greece were placed by the classroom window, and Markino's first task was to do charcoal drawings of their necks. The teachers came round for 14-15 minutes a day. After two or three months Markino advanced to a class where he drew full-length portraits of the ancient sculptures and then on to the nude class. The fee for the alabaster class was $6 a month, for the nude class it was $7. Markino was then working at the home of May Holden, a student in a higher grade, but with wages of $2.50 a week, he found it difficult to find money for materials and living expenses. Fortunately, the nude class was 1pm–5pm, so in the mornings he decided to do work such as window cleaning.

In his second year, Markino concentrated on landscape painting, and with a classmate, Mary McClean, he went out into the suburbs and sketched the views: the steep cliffs of the Pacific: the wild poppies of Richmond Plateau; the eucalyptus trees at the Golden Gate Bridge and the dells of Oakland. Winter in the San Francisco area was comparatively warm and the air rose warm and hazy, making it appear as though a transparent silk veil

INTRODUCTION

covered the scenery. He tried to paint this mysterious silk veil, first with oils, then using pastels and then with watercolour materials, but to no avail. Then Markino experimented with mixing various mediums. In doing so he chanced on an important discovery. In his autobiography, *Idle Dreams*, Markino wrote, 'I can achieve a very soft colour by mixing in oils the strongest primary colour with its opponent colour. Newman is the best make for mixing the watercolour carmine with another colour. I made many other discoveries and was able to achieve some sense of light when trying to draw the silk veil. When framed in black this looks like the silk veil'.

Although Markino struggled to give expression to the silk veil during his stay in San Francisco, he met with no noticeable success. However, it is certain that these efforts provided the groundwork for the paintings which gave him the nickname 'Heiji, painter of fog', in London. Two pieces of bad news reached him during his time at the Art School. The first was news of his father's death on 4 May 1895. The other was a letter from his aunt announcing Maki Hotta's marriage in October of 1896. Swiftly following this was the news, four months later, of Maki's sudden death on 4 February.

Markino had intended to return home during a break in his studies, but having lost his father and Maki, he no longer had any desire to return. He decided rather to go to New York and await an opportunity to travel to Europe. Intending to keep himself in New York by doing illustrations for newspapers and magazines, he began learning pen and ink drawing. He also got work making false teeth; the time spent helping at his cousin's Toyama Dental Surgery while he was in Nagoya was proving useful.

In about June 1897, he was invited to the home of his classmate Kate Scott, in Oakland. Her father was a retired naval captain and had in his gallery works by

INTRODUCTION

artists such as Renoir, Gainsborough, Hogarth, Turner, Whistler, Millais and Corot. Scott introduced Markino to the Japanese Navy Ship Commissioner Shozo Sakurai. Sakurai recommended that he go to Paris to study art and promised him an introduction to the owner of an antique shop in the Rue de la Victoire, Tadamasa Hayashi. On 14 August 1897, seen off by Captain Scott, McClean, Maria and Sakurai, Markino put America behind him after a stay of four years and one month.

Departure for Paris

In mid-August 1897, Markino boarded a cross-continental express in Oakland, bound for New York. The train went through Sacramento and Omaha and stopped overnight in Chicago, where he walked by Lake Michigan and saw the works of the great European and American artists in the museums. From Detroit, he crossed into Canada and marvelled at the size and splendour of the Niagara Falls. In New York, he stayed at the Japanese Club at 3 Sand Street in Brooklyn, and began to study French conversation, while helping to edit the Japanese newspaper *New York Shuho*, owned by M. Matsumoto. Here he also met Kazuchika Okura of the Japanese shop Morimura Shoten and the watercolour artist, Katsumi Miyake. In his autobiography *Omoizuru mama*, Miyake writes, 'When, for some reason, I dropped into the Japanese Club one day, I met a young artist who had arrived from San Francisco 2-3 days before . . . His name was Yoshio Markino, and it transpired that, while working in San Francisco, he had fallen in love with an American girl, to whom he was engaged, and that he was on his way to Paris where they were to study art together . . . Markino spoke openly about his love, just as in a novel. To anyone who would listen, he explained that he was going on ahead and that his fiancée would

INTRODUCTION

join him later. However, in reality Markino's love life was not so happy. It seems that, when he was in Hong Kong, he did indeed become engaged to the daughter of an American who loved art, but that the girl's father was shocked at her love for a Jap. Markino went into exile, saying he was going to study in Paris'. The girl mentioned here was probably Kate Scott.

On 8 November, Markino left for France in the third class of a steamship, departing from West Houston on the Hudson River and arriving in Le Havre after a week's voyage. There he boarded a train for Paris. Markino went to the Rue de la Victoire to see Tadamasa Hayashi, the art dealer to whom Shozo Sakurai had given him an introduction, but unfortunately Hayashi had returned to Japan to prepare for the Exposition to be held in Paris in 1900. Having no alternative, Markino stayed for a while at the Suwa Hotel in Rue Lafayette, which had been recommended to him, and saw the sights of Paris.

Construction work on the Grand Palais and the Alexandre III Bridge was at its height. May Holden, who was living in Rue Petit Notre Dame in the Latin Quarter, and other older students from Hopkins who were then in Paris, welcomed Heiji warmly and showed him the Jardin du Luxembourg, the Louvre and other sights. He also met the watercolourist Saburosuke Okada (1869–1939), who was studying in Paris, and from whom he heard the latest news from the Japanese art world. However, he was discouraged by the unexpected absence of Hayashi and was also running short of money. At this point, Markino wrote to Umataro Ide, who had been at Hopkins before him, to seek his advice and immediately received a reply urging him to join him in London. He therefore resolved to go to London rather than stay in Paris, where he had difficulties with the language. He did not have quite enough for the fare, so Shoichiro, son of Munenori Terashima, lent him 10 francs. He boarded a

INTRODUCTION

ship for England, arrived in New Haven six hours later and, early on 8 December, took his first steps towards London. Markino then was 27 years old and about to embark on the experiences so vividly portrayed in *A Japanese Artist in London*.

After A Japanese Artist in London

Around 1910, when this book was published, watercolour artists such as Ikunosuke Shirataki, Kunzo Minami, Wakun Ishibashi, Chuzo Matsuyama and Takezo Sato were studying in London. Markino met Sato a few times and it seems strange that he did not actively seek out the other artists. He was to spend 40 years in London and his struggle to find acceptance in the British art world is related in this book. The early part of his stay in the UK is therefore known in some detail. However, less is known of the 32 years which follow before he left the country, other than the series of eight articles written for the Tokyo *Asahi Shimbun*, and manuscripts submitted to the magazine *Kaizo*, which were finally published in one volume in Japanese, *Taiei Yonjunen Konjaku Monogatari* (*Forty Years of My Life in England*).

Return to Japan and Later Years

Japan declared war on the UK and America on 8 December 1941, and on 27 September the following year, Markino returned to Japan after an absence of 50 years, on the repatriation ship *Tatsuta Maru*. On his return, Markino stayed with the Shigemitsus in Tokyo's Kojimachi, but after the house was burned down in an air raid in May 1945, he moved with them for a while to Nikko. When the family moved to Zaimokuza, in Kamakura at the end of the year, Markino went with them. He continued his studies of German, French, Italian, Span-

INTRODUCTION

ish and Russian, going out to sketch in his free time as a change of scene. Markino was often visited by Yone Noguchi, who had shared his lodgings in London, Shintaro Ryu, Tatsuo Mitarai and Junichi Hitomi.

In 1952, he had a one-man show at Tokyo International Club, having been proposed by Mamoru Shigemitsu and Fumio Asakura, where he sold most of his work. With the money thus earned, he left the family he was staying with at the time (the Yamamotos) and was forgotten for some years. Markino lived in an apartment nearby, but had soon spent the money from the exhibition through wasteful living and, in 1955, was discovered in a ramshackle house in Yamanouchi, Kamakura, in a piteous state near to starvation. He was 85 years old. With slogans such as 'Don't forget the ageing great artist', his hometown Koromo began a goodwill movement to help him. Their efforts were to no avail and Markino died the following year, on 18 October 1956. Mrs Yoshi Suzuki, who lived in Kamakura and had looked after the artist in his last years, was leaving the Akizuki Hospital after visiting Markino. Descending the hospital steps, she chanced to look behind her and saw a dead leaf falling. Struck by a sudden premonition, she returned to the ward to find that it was as she had feared.

It may seem that Markino, who had enjoyed such acclaim in England, had a very sad and lonely old age. However, to me, he seems to have had a wonderful and fulfilled life, continuing to study as he wished until he was satisfied.

Markino and Anglo–Japanese Relations

This then was what I subsequently discovered about the life of the writer whose book I first read in that pub near the British Museum 15 years ago. I have poor eyesight, so luckily for me the book was easy to read because it had

INTRODUCTION

a large typeface and the lines were widely spaced. Even in flattery, you would not say that the English was good. But this book, written in Markino's own colloquial Japanese English style became required reading. As you continue to read, you may find that there are parts at which tears will fall unbidden, but that there are other instances where he presents a trivial matter casually and with humour. I felt that this was an unique book which skilfully blended pathos with humour. The part which made the deepest impression on me is in Chapter 12 'My Japanese Friends' and is Markino's own honest feeling: '... in England I always feel I am an interpreter between English and Japanese, and I want to introduce to all the English readers the different morals of Japanese peoples'. When I read this I felt that Yoshio Markino was the first exponent of Anglo–Japanese cultural exchange – an internationalist in the true sense of the word. I do not have the talent of Markino, who in *My Recollections and Reflections* (published 1913) and *When I Was a Child* (published 1912) introduces the Japanese concept of *Bushido* (way of the warrior) while telling of his childhood, or who draws pictures evocative of the atmosphere of *Ukiyo-e* (Pictures of the Floating World). Furthermore, sadly, I do not even have the English ability to explain the morality of the Japanese as Markino did. However, I felt that I should like to do something, however small, to further Anglo–Japanese cultural exchange.

The insignificant outcome of this is the Soseki Museum in London which I opened in 1984 at my own expense. If I had not come across this book, I should probably simply have remained one more lover of Soseki Natsume's literature and would never have dreamt of opening the Soseki Museum in London. The contrast between Markino's and Soseki's experience of London is stark. Yoshio Markino lived in England for almost half a

INTRODUCTION

century; had a positive attitude, became integrated into English society and wrote many books in English; and made English people aware of Japanese morals and ideology. Soseki Natsume lived in London for two years; hardly went out except to receive private lessons from Mr Craig; was earnestly absorbed in the study of English literature; returned to Japan and wrote novels while teaching at Tokyo University; and conveyed, not just English literature, but the concept of 'individualism'. Making these two the cornerstones of the Soseki Museum, I hope to introduce the forerunners of Japanese students overseas who lived in obscurity and have still not achieved full recognition in Japan.

Sammy Ikuo Tsunematsu

Acknowledgements

I should like to express my sincere gratitude to Hiroshi Makino; grandson of Yoshio Markino's elder brother, Toshitaro, who has given permission for the reprint of this book in 1991, 81 years after the publication of the original, and, appropriately, on the 100th anniversary of the [London] Japan Society with which Markino was connected. I should also like to acknowledge and thank many friends and acquaintances for their assistance with this, albeit brief, introduction. In particular, Professor Ross Kilpatrick of Queen's University, Canada, who has always generously provided me with new materials for my research on Markino; Mr Hideo Sekiguchi, Headmaster of the Teikyo School, London; Professor Shinichi Miyazawa, Saitama Women's Junior College, and the many other individuals and organizations who have helped me: Mr Sadao Oba, Mr Akio Sato, Professor Shuichi Iwatsubo, Professor Saburo Minagawa, Mr Hiroaki Matsuyama, Dr Yasue and Kyoko Tanaka, Mr Katsuo Tamura, Mr Yasushi Asaoka, Ms Tomoko Ito, Professor Tetsuro Murata, Dr John Clark, Mr John Shepherds, Mr Jeffrey Somers, Sir Hugh Cortazzi, Dr Carmen Blacker, Ms Heidi Potter, Mr Tsutomu Tabata, Mr and Mrs Tony and Keiko Lessing, the British Library, the Colindale Newspaper Library, Westminster Library, Somerset House, Catherine House. My thanks also to Alastair Dingwall and John Edmondson of In Print Publishing, who agreed to publish this book.

Finally, my thanks to my dear wife, Yoshiko and son Mikio. Yoshiko has tirelessly supported me in my research on Markino, even though she sees no end to it.

Sammy Ikuo Tsunematsu

A Japanese Artist
in
London

To

Mr. and Mrs. M. H. Spielmann

AN APPRECIATION

By DOUGLAS SLADEN

This seems to me to be a book of unique interest. The irresistible humour and the force of Yoshio Markino's writing is well known to critics, for in reviewing his three large colour books, "The Colour of London," "The Colour of Paris," and "The Colour of Rome," most of them have given as much space to the single chapter contributed by the artist as they have to the entire letterpress of the book.

Nor is this surprising, for Mr. Markino in his quaint English has sometimes an arrestiveness almost equal to Thomas Carlyle's. There is real style in it. He has evolved a grammar of his own which is strikingly effective.

In his new volume, "A Japanese Artist in London," he has a subject eminently suited to exhibit the humour and pathos and forcefulness of his style. For in it he relates his stern

AN APPRECIATION

battles with starvation, and the strange experiences into which he was plunged by the extraordinary succession of trades to which his poverty condemned him. When he first came over he was working in the Japanese Legation and Art Schools. Then he tried starvation for a time. He became a model in one of the Art Schools where he had been a student; then a tombstone-maker at Norwood. Then he starved again until he met his good fairy, Mr. M. H. Spielmann, who got him various commissions. He helped to stage "The Darling of the Gods"; illustrated magazines and newspapers, not at all in his own line; and finally obtained a commission to illustrate "The Colour of London," and arranged an exhibition where he sold the originals.

In San Francisco he cleaned windows and scrubbed floors to get the money for his art-school fees, and lived on the bread given to the students to rub out the charcoal; then he made teeth for a dentist; at odd times he has been even a naval architect.

He belongs to a very old Samurai family in Japan, and always kept his starvation and hard-

AN APPRECIATION

ships concealed from them with true Japanese Bushido. But now the world is to have the full and unvarnished account of them told in Mr. Markino's inimitable Japanese English—and the result is a book of pathos and humour which comes half-way between Michael Fairless's "Roadmender" and Mr. Dooley's Impressions.

It is a book which will live, for it tells, with absolute candour and fidelity, of life right down to the bed-rock of starvation, and it adds a new variety of humour to British literature.

The book was not easily written. It perhaps never would have been written if so much of it had not been comprised in his correspondence with Miss Olave Potter, who wrote the letterpress of "The Colour of Rome." Some of the matter which is here made public he wrote in his letters to her, other parts of it were written from her suggestions. Sometimes Mr. Markino was at a loss for the English word. He replaced it with a picture, going back to the Japanese habit of ideograms, and so ingeniously that Miss Potter

AN APPRECIATION

was never at a loss to translate it into words. She arranged the manuscript and corrected the proofs. How wisely she refrained from tampering with his English, the reader will see. Its very crudeness has its force, its humour, and not unfrequently its pathos; while its artless confessions show that Mr. Markino has as white a soul as ever entered a human body. He is absolutely candid and entirely without false shame; he records poverty so dire that his work was paralysed by hunger. He often had to get into bed in the middle of the day to get warm enough to hold his brushes, and at one time walked every day from Kensal Rise to Norwood, except a pennyworth of tram from Westminster to Brixton, and from Norwood back the whole way to Kensal Rise, which he reached at midnight.

There are no pages which make pleasanter reading than those which record the goodness of the poor landladies to this Japanese castaway; when he could not afford to buy food they shared their own with him; when he had no money at all they let his bill for lodgings

AN APPRECIATION

run into pounds. Some went further and lent him the money out of their savings-boxes. When prosperity shone again a little they were always faithfully repaid. He writes of them now in the same terms of equality and friendship as he uses when he is talking about his Cabinet Minister friend. He is as incapable of thinking himself better than the humble as he is of considering himself inferior to the great. At the present moment he shares his heart between the Cabinet Minister and a shoemaker.

Yoshio Markino is more like a spirit than most of the spirits clothed in flesh which we call human beings. At houses where he opens his heart to their inmates and feels intimate, he flutters in bubbling over with news and excitement—he always has news even if he has met them an hour ago—he counts his friends, as it were, to see if they are all there, gathers each to himself with some little private personal touch, and then sits down on the floor as he was taught to sit when he was a tiny mite in Dai Nippon. His unselfishness, his chivalry, his warmth of heart recall all one has read of the

AN APPRECIATION

Bushido of the Samurai class, to which he belongs, in the Tales of Old Japan. And every reader of these pages will see much of the magical personality, of which I speak, reflected in them. These lines, written by I don't know whom, might have been written of him—

> " He was the proper, friend-making, everywhere friend-finding soul,
> Fit for the sunshine, so it followed him,
> A happy-tempered bringer of the best out of the worst."

PREFACE

Just the moment I was going to start writing this book, one of my intimate Japanese friends—Wakamiya—has sent me the first number of his new periodical. There was one page entitled " Human Voices and Devil Voices." I saw these words on the page: " All humans are born in this world with crying voice: the beginning of human life is Trouble. All humans go into coffins with the voice of praying: the end of human life is Repentance. . . . It is not hard to make the whole world an enemy, but it is hard indeed to make the bakers good friends. . . . Poverty is the most final weakness."

My friend has conquered me. What single word could I add to this ? It is only for a few weeks that baby birds enjoy their comfortable life while they are sleeping under their mother's warm breast in the nest. At this time they may desire not to meet rains, snows, and frosts all through their life. But is there any single bird in this world which escapes the storms ?

PREFACE

So with our life. Go to the peers and ask them their life; they will tell you their sad life-story, which may easily make you shed your tears. Go to cabmen, ask their life-story, you may still more easily be moved to tears with their pathetic stories.

I myself have had some experiences in the last thirteen years in London. And now I have to write this out. But the readers please kindly remember I do not mean to be so conceited to be proud of my little experiences; neither do I grumble, especially before such a wonderful nation like the Britons, whose perseverance in hardship is simply marvellous. Indeed, they were my leaders all through my hard life, and I am much indebted to their encouragement.

My life is as simple and unworthy as my pictures. The matter of fact is, my publishers demanded me to write down all my experiences, so if only the readers don't yawn on my writing, my publishers and I shall be very grateful.

It was rather a difficult task for me to go on for whole book with my terribly deformed English, but my English friend has so kindly dragged me all round to reach the finishing point. If it were a Marathon race I should not be entitled the prize like Dorando.

I think there are two kinds of life in this

PREFACE

world—Safety in Danger, and Danger in Safety. For instance, a baby in his mother's arms is frightened by dogs on the ground. That is danger in safety. A swindler on a soft and comfortable sofa is safety in danger. My life belonged to the former.

Analysis of my life.

Discouraged? Very often.

Disappointed? Always.

Spoilt? Very much by John Bulls and John Bullesses.

In short, I have always been mentally pleasant and financially unpleasant. But I am told by my elder English friends that my financial unpleasantness was all through my own fault.

When I was a boy at home I was rather spoilt, because my father was very generous to the villagers. I was called the Hon. little Master of Markino. Here, in London, I have no reason whatever to be spoilt. Why are all my English friends so good to me? I must put all this down as the great generosity of the good Britons.

A JAPANESE ARTIST IN LONDON

CHAPTER I

MY ARRIVAL IN ENGLAND

It was December 8, 1897, when I arrived here from America, where I had been some four and a half years. I was quite young, but I was far more boyish than my own age. First of all I went to Paris, where I wanted to study Art. But I had neither money nor any knowledge of the French language. I had only one recommendation letter to some one. Unfortunately this gentleman had left Paris previously, so I decided to come to London to see some of my Japanese friends. I took the night train through Dieppe and New Heaven (Haven). From the very first it seemed to me to be a New Heaven; I had such a good impression with England. Those English officers on board the Channel boats had such gentle

A JAPANESE ARTIST IN LONDON

faces; they talked to me so kindly. It was a great comfort after the desperate struggle in Paris, where I was practically dumb and deaf.

When I arrived at New Heaven I had only forty francs in my pocket, and one small bag which contained three collars, one white shirt, one necktie, two pairs of socks, a German Bible and Keigan (a Buddhist Philosophy by Colonel Torio). The custom-house officer was so surprised when I told him that it was all my possessions.

It was four or five in the morning. I went into a coffee-stall and had a cup. The man said it was "thruppence." I could not understand it. I gave him ten-franc piece, and he gave me the change. I could not, of course, count it, but after arriving in London my Japanese friend saw the change and he said it was quite right. The English money is so difficult for foreigners to calculate. For about half-year or so I always used to give bigger coin than the price of the things I purchased, and take the change without examining it. I was never deceived. Only I had to have so many coppers in my pocket—sometimes over three shillings in coppers!

Now, coming back to my journey. I arrived at London Bridge at seven, and took another train to Greenwich, where my Japanese artist

MY ARRIVAL IN ENGLAND

friend was staying. I had another recommendation letter to the Japanese Naval Attaché in London. I saw him immediately. He was only too glad to keep me as his private secretary, for at the time Japan had ordered from English shipbuilders warships and some twenty or thirty torpedo boats, and he was extraordinarily busy. The naval inspector's office was in Gloucester Terrace, so I settled myself down at 4 Milner Street in Chelsea. From ten to six I had to work at the office, then I attended at South Kensington College of Science and Art at night. My wages at the office were £5 a month; later on £8, then £9. I learnt afterwards that all this was from the naval attaché's own pocket, just to "keep me on for the sake of art study." I was quite alone in some boudoir-like room to work for the attaché. My surprise there on the first day was that the landlady brought me tea and bread and butter at 4.30. I said to myself, what a kind lady she is! The next day she brought in the tea again. So the third day I asked her if that tea was from the attaché or from her, and why? She said it was English custom to have afternoon tea. Oh, what a beautiful custom! It was really a great refreshing for me. I said, "I quite love England, only for afternoon tea alone."

A JAPANESE ARTIST IN LONDON

At this time I began to stroll on Sunday afternoons. At first I was so frightened with London fogs. I thought, if I live in such dreadful fog I will soon become consumptive. So I bought a respirator at a drug store, and used to wear it whenever I went out. When I visited peoples they laughed at me because I got a round black mark round my mouth. Nevertheless I kept it on until some doctor told me the fog was not so injurious as I thought. (Who knows? This "dreadful fog" has become my greatest fascination, only a few years later!)

As I had been in America previously for four years, naturally I used to compare everything here with that of America; and what great contrast between the two countries—especially to a Japanese! Here I feel I need to talk about my life in America, just roughly.

I ran away from home to San Francisco on July 1893, with a hope to become a poet or a writer in English. All my friends there advised me to become an artist instead, because one cannot master a foreign language. So I entered into Hopkin's Art College. Of course I was penniless. I had to make livelihood by washing windows and dishes, or a little better thing, making sets of false teeth for some dentists. It was awfully difficult for me to

MY ARRIVAL IN ENGLAND

pay my school tuition, seven dollars a month. I stayed there for four years, but practically I have not attended the school more than twelve months altogether. The school used to supply French breads to the students for the purpose of charcoal drawing. But I used to live on this bread. I made it as my luncheon every day. (This is the very first time that I confess the truth. Thank Heaven that the curator did not find out!)

I was rather amused with my poor life, but by no means did I feel pleasant with the way those Californians treated me. It is the world-known fact that they hate Japanese. While I have been there four years I never went out to the parks, for I was so frightened of those savage people, who threw stones and bricks at me. Even when I was walking on the street the showers of pebbles used to fall upon me often. And I was spat on more occasionally. Of course they were very low-class peoples, but even better-class peoples had not a very nice manner to the Japanese. If I got into tram-car and sat down on an empty seat beside some ladies, they used to glare at me with such disgusting expression, and would get up and go away to find out a seat far away from me.

Once I went into a cable car in Sutter Street.

A JAPANESE ARTIST IN LONDON

I saw my classmate young lady opposite me. I took my hat off and greeted her. She turned her face away. I could not understand why, as she used to be so intimate to me in the class-room. The next day I went to the school. As soon as she saw me she began to apologise me, saying it was not her idea at all to insult me, but she was so frightened that those other occupants of the car might be indignant with her speaking to a Japanese. Another time I experienced far worse thing. I went out with my paint-box and canvas to the beach near Cliff House. No sooner than I started to paint, several boys came to me. They were all older than myself. They broke my paint-box. They threw away all colours and brushes into the sea and tore my canvas. Then they fled away. I was such a helpless boy I could do nothing but weep on the spot for hours. I was so sad, because it took me three or four months working very hard to buy those materials.

Such was my life in America. But I had not so bad a feeling then as I should surely have if it happened now! Because America was the first foreign country I ever visited in my life, so I thought, if we Japanese go out anywhere we shall be treated like that, as an inferior race.

MY ARRIVAL IN ENGLAND

After such experiences I was naturally surprised with the cosmopolitan ideas of the Londoners.

I started my first sightseeing from Hyde Park and the Green Park and St. James's Park. I could not understand all those iron railings. I thought they were to divide private grounds from the public ones. But I saw many people on both sides. I so timidly walked inside the rail. Nobody shouted me. Then I went near the crowds of people with still more fear. Being quite ignorant of the English civilisation I anticipated some pebble-showers every minute. I waited and waited with beating heart, but nothing happened to me at all. I walked into the crowds who were feeding birds in the lake of St. James's Park. Nobody spat on me! I ventured myself into the thickest crowds, and I was squeezed between the peoples. Nobody took any notice of me. "Hallo, hallo, what's matter?" I said in my heart. "Perhaps they don't know I am a Japanese." I took off my hat on purpose to show my black hair. Finally one man pushed me quite accidentally, and he touched his hand to his hat and apologised me very politely. I realised at last that I was in the country where I could enjoy my liberty quite freely. Fancy polite apology instead of swearing and spitting! I

A JAPANESE ARTIST IN LONDON

felt as if I had come to a paradise in this world, and I was quite melted with comfort.

Perhaps nobody could ever imagine my most grateful feeling at this moment, except those of my fellow-country friends who were in California once. Even now, after some thirteen years' stay in London, I often have nightmares of California, and wake up in midnight and wonder where I really am. When I realise that I am in London I feel so happy.

In the streets first thing I noticed was so many silk hats. Then those people who were walking seemed to me so gentle, and with very dignified manners. Indeed, in California you cannot walk one block without hearing swearings. Here you hear apologising words instead.

On the bus I often sat down by the side of English lady. When other peoples got off there were many empty seats, but she would not bother herself to remove. In fact, it would give me more comfortable seat to be alone, but the idea of English ladies not bothering to move was far greater comfort for me.

At this time I went to a little newspaper shop to buy a box of cigarettes. The shopkeeper treated me quite same way with his countrymen. I asked him if he has seen Japanese before. He said "No." Then I asked him again if he was not curious of me?

MY ARRIVAL IN ENGLAND

He said, " No, sir. You see, sir, we 'ave our colonies all *hover* the world, sir—white men, yellow men, brown men and black men are forming parts of the British nation, so I am not curious of a Japanese gentleman at all."

What a broad mind he had! He was only a little shopkeeper, but he was worthy of being called one of the most civilised of the nations. I made a friendship with him at once, and I told him how I was treated in California. He said, "Thut ain't fair, sir! Indeed, thut ain't fair!" How sweet this word was to me! I carried this sweet "thut ain't fair" in my head, and slept with it all night so comfortably.

As I lived in Chelsea I used to have walk on the Chelsea Embankment. It was my favourite place; so it is now too. One afternoon I made a longer promenade along the embankment to Westminster. On the way, I saw a large stone building in a peculiar shape, the Britannia on the top of the roof. It had no window. It stood dead silent like a ghost in the evening mist. I thought it must be a mausoleum of some ancient kings. But my landlady told me that it must be the Tate Gallery. "You ought to go in there one day, there are beautiful pictures; it is just the place you ought to go to."

Westminster Abbey was a great revelation

A JAPANESE ARTIST IN LONDON

to me. While I was a schoolboy in Japan, I learnt all the history of the Abbey; then Washington Irving described it so vividly in his "Sketch Book," which was my most favourite book. Generally travellers are disappointed with sightseeing if they trust books too much. But Westminster to me was the reverse. I not only realised every word that Irving said, but I found the Abbey more solemn, more dignified, and more sacred than I was imagining. Those numerous white marble statues of the great statesmen are in just the right place. They seem to tell me all that they have done. I feel myself so small and so humble before them. And those chapels and chantrys of Henry VII. are something like a dream of the past history. Even now if I go there I forget all my worldly care.

To my Japanese eyes the building looks far older than its history tells. In Japan stones almost two thousand years old are not worn out like this. Perhaps it is through the English climate. But surely everything English doesn't always look older? For instance, look at the English women. First of all, Her Majesty the Queen looks so young. I cannot believe her age. Some Japanese naval officer attended a levée. He told me he had the honour to speak to Her Majesty while she

MY ARRIVAL IN ENGLAND

was Princess of Wales. He was quite near to her, and he had the same idea with me—it was impossible to believe her age. I know several English ladies who look like their daughter's sisters. It is true what I heard in Japan. "English women are flowers all their life." I wonder is that through the climate too? My logic seems rather poor in this instance.

I have quite forgotten to tell my most important thing—my art-study at South Kensington. There I studied casts with charcoal until March of the next year, 1898, and during this time I used to go to Greenwich every Sunday to see my Japanese friend. He was studying the designs at Goldsmith Institute in New Cross. I envied him so much. He had plenty of friends at the Institute, and such a homely life at his diggings. He told me English peoples never become friends without introduction. If I only decided to attend the night class of Goldsmith Institute he would introduce me to all his English friends. Then his landlady, too, persuaded me to come to live with them. I was only too delighted. I came back to my place in Milner Street and told the landlady I was going to remove on the same day. She was so astonished, and explained me it was the English custom to give one week's notice. Here I learnt another lesson of English life. I felt myself a savage, and was ashamed so much.

But I could not control myself for a long week to wait, so I gave a full week payment to her and said, "All the same, I shall go." She would not accept that. She said, "Give me only half of that, as you did not know our custom"; and she told me with moisted eyes that she would miss me very much. In fact, I had quite comfortable life there. She had taken care of me very kindly. It was my pleasure every night when I came back from the school to see my window lit up with the firelight inside, and to find a hot bottle in my bed. I was quite sad when I shook her hand for good-bye.

But when I arrived at Mazehill Station I forgot everything, and was so excited about my new home. Everybody was surprised when I arrived at the house. They never thought I would come so soon. My bed was not even ready yet. When I told them what I had done they were all very angry with my rashness, especially because I was so poor—£5 a month!

CHAPTER II

MY LIFE IN GREENWICH

My new home was No. 96 Annandale Road, quite close to Mazehill Station. It was a little two-storey house, a regular suburban type. My room was at the back of the house; such a tiny room that when they put in a single bed, a wash-stand and a desk, I could hardly move. Underneath my window was a cemetery. There were a few trees. Every morning at dawn a blackbird used to sing on the top of a tree. It was first time in my life to hear blackbirds. They have such a beautiful voice, and I was so happy to be awakened by them in the morning. My landlady told me that one of the blackbirds laid eggs on that tree, so the husband bird sang every morning to please his wife bird. Then she said, "You see, in England husbands always take great care of their wives. Even the blackbirds do so. If you marry in England you must do the same." I was so amused with that.

My Japanese friend took me to Goldsmith

A JAPANESE ARTIST IN LONDON

Institute in the evenings, where I was introduced to the teachers—Mr. Marriott and Mr. Buckman in Life Class, and Mr. Firn in Design Class. I belonged to Mr. Marriott's class, and started the life study.

On Sunday, my Japanese friend and I used to go to Plumstead and Shooter's Hill. With the latter I was quite familiar when I read Charles Dickens' "Tale of Two Cities," and I recollected that story of the Highlander as if it were really happening.

The time came when my Japanese friend had to go back to Japan, but I still stayed in the same house and enjoyed my homely life all the same. The landlord's name was Mr. Watson. He was a collector of the Prudential Life Assurance Company. He was about sixty years old, and he had such a benevolent-looking face, like that famous picture of Sir John Millais' "Victory, O Lord." He had beautiful long grey beard and whiskers. His gentle and tender eyes were sunk in his face. They were so tender, especially when he smiled. I used to call him "Moses," and made him as my model to study "the old English man" whenever he and I both had time. His wife was only thirty-two or thirty-three, very jolly and extraordinarily kind-hearted woman. She used to come into my room every day when

MY LIFE IN GREENWICH

I was out, and brush my clothes and make "order" inside of my drawers. First time in my life since I left home that all my socks and underwears were mended! She took a great trouble of shopping "something" especially for my suppers every day, and after hard work at the office and hard study at the school these suppers were great treats for me.

They had two daughters—Elsie and Winnie. The elder was eleven and the younger was eight. They both were very pretty girls. Elsie was very affectionate and rather shy; she used to like to read and play the piano. Winnie was rather like a Persian cat, and petted by everybody. She had such big round blue eyes like owl's, and beautiful curls of chocolate hair, and a fresh complexion. She looked really like a doll. I often tried to draw her portrait, but it was too difficult for me. She was my idol! These two girls used to sit on my both sides, and were "so earnest to hear some stories about abroad." I used to tell them about Japan, Sandwich Islands, and America. One day I told them how beautiful were those Californian wild poppies growing on a vast field. They wanted to go there. I said, "But there is a most dangerous thing there. It is a poisonous snake called Rattlesnake. If this snake bites people, they die immediately. Only the way to escape death from this terrible snake is to cut off the part where it bit. If that snake bite my hand I would cut off my hand at once ; if it were my feet, I would cut off my feet."

The children looked at me with some curious expression. They both were quite silent for a while. Elsie broke out first. " If that snake bites your head, would you cut off your own head at once ? "

I could not answer.

Winnie was very serious, and said, " Elsie, don't ask such a question. If Mr. Markino cut off his head he could not come to live with us." Elsie was quite sorry. I took both heads of these angel-like, innocent English children under my two arms, and kissed them most tenderly.

I must mention another instance to show how the younger girl was attached to me, and what a curio-comic girl she was. One evening, I was so tired and dull. The landlady said, " Mr. Markino, I suppose you have got a cold, you need some mixture." By this she meant whisky. But Winnie was listening, and immediately she ran out of doors. After a few minutes she came back and threw a little packet at me, and said, " 'Ere you are ! " It was a real mixture for a cold. I learnt afterwards

MY LIFE IN GREENWICH

that she went to a chemist and bought it with her own money.

Saturdays were their "great days." All other week-days I had to leave the house before they got up, so that I could reach the office in time after the train and bus journey from Mazehill to Gloucester Terrace; and they were generally in bed when I went back after the school. I had no chance to see them on those days. On Saturdays the office closed half day. I used to buy oranges or apples at Charing Cross Station and put them in my pockets. They were always waiting me at the Mazehill Station. They often waited two or three hours there when I was too busy at the office. Soon as I got off the train they would search all my pockets and find out "something." Then they were so happy. I used to carry Winnie on my back, while Elsie pulled my coat to guide me to home. If I had an early afternoon I used to take them to London to see Zoo, Parks, or some music halls. They were too frightened of traffics to cross the road; I used to carry them in my arms, one each time, to the other side. We spent Sundays generally at Greenwich Park. They were so proud to their children friends because they had walk with a Japanese "gentleman." What a different thought from those Californian children!

A JAPANESE ARTIST IN LONDON

The landlady used to say to me, "Oh, Mr. Markino, please don't spoil my children so. I don't know what will become of them after all this."

At this time I wrote all my London life to some Japanese friends in San Francisco. They all envied me much.

I stayed at this most comfortable home for about a year and a half. Then that poor old Watson died. His wife was so upset. She could not survive more than half a year and died, leaving those poor children alone in this world. I was obliged to remove to a new diggings at New Cross. I was no less sad than those poor children.

They had some rich relative among the English Navy. This naval officer sent them to a boarding-school. Since then I did not hear of them for such a long time. Just the time when "The Colour of London" was published in 1907, I found a letter addressed to my publishers, with a Canadian stamp on it. It was from Winnie. She told me in her letter that soon after she and her sister finished the school, they both went to St. John, where their aunt was. She wanted to write me so often, but did not know my address. At last, to her delight, she saw some reviews of my book in a paper, and she hurried to write to me.

MY LIFE IN GREENWICH

I answered her immediately, asking her if she would like some toy-books. I got her answer like this: "My dear Mr. Markino, you cannot imagine how delighted I was to hear from you after all. I am afraid you are still thinking of me as a little 'Toby' in a pinafore. But remember, I am seventeen, and I believe I am a few inches taller than you now. . . ."

One of her photographs came with this letter. Indeed, she was quite a handsome young lady! How wonderful Time passes by so quick! If my art could grow up at the same rate as this little friend, I should be a great master by this time!

A few weeks later I got another letter from her, saying that she had "a nice young man with a very kind heart," &c. &c. She asked my advice whether to marry or not. I persuaded her to marry. A wedding-card came to me half a year later! Alas, my own art is not in the stage of marriage yet!

Elsie, the elder girl, began to write to me too. In all her letters she expressed how happy she was in Canada. Last Christmas she sent me a beautifully bound book of Longfellow, with these words on the frontispage—"Recollecting all your kindness long, long ages ago."

CHAPTER III

MY LIFE IN NEW CROSS

In New Cross I lived in two places. First in Amersham Road, and then at St. Donald Road. I have nothing much to say of these two places. I had apartments, and took all meals in my own room, so I did not see much of the landlords or their families. The second place was awfully cheap—11s. 6d. for a week.

At this time the Japanese Naval office was moved to Victoria Street. I used to walk from Charing Cross to the office way round St. James's Park. It was so nice to see that pretty bit of the Park every day, but that was not my real reason. I tried to avoid seeing Westminster Abbey too often. I shall give the reader full reason for this in the words which my father used to tell me when I was a boy. He was a great pilgrim to visit all historical places in Japan, in order to make poetries. He said, " We have most poetic feeling in our minds when we only read books of those places and don't visit them at all.

MY LIFE IN NEW CROSS

Generally we are disappointed if we see the places actually. Sometimes they are more poetic than we were imagining, but even then, if we visit the same places too often and become too familiar with them our poetic ideals suffer a great deal."

I thoroughly agree with my father. In the case of Westminster Abbey it was "more poetic than I was imagining," but I was so afraid to get too familiar with it. That was why I tried not to see it every day. Even now, I visit it quite seldom, once in three months or so. Then every time I enjoy myself there with some singular sorts of feelings.

In the evening, after the office, I used to take the same train from Charing Cross to New Cross with Mr. Marriott and Mr. Buckman. Both were my teachers at life class. They were very kind gentlemen, and I made a great friendship with them. They used to invite me to their musical evenings. At the school I had about seven or eight class-mates. Some of them had awfully lucky names for artists—Leighton, Watts, or Prior, something like that. But my most intimate class-mates were Sand, Galleghar, and Jennings.

Sand was a boy of a bootmaker at Catford. He was the youngest, about seventeen or

A JAPANESE ARTIST IN LONDON

eighteen. As his manner was rather rough, all other students used to mock at him. But I always had a great sympathy with him. He was such a simple boy, and was so earnest to study hard. He was very ambitious too.

One evening all students had a "chat." I said, "If I become quite well-known artist some day . . ." They all laughed at me. But Sand came to me and shook my hand warmly (if roughly too): "Never mind their laughter, my Chin-Chin; you and I shall make 'a name' some day." I wonder what has become of this ambitious boy now, after some ten years? I would not be surprised if I see his name big somewhere one of these days.

Galleghar was an Irish. He was very philosophical, and his pen-and-ink sketches of trees on commons were full of poetry. But he was such a woman-hater. I heard a great deal of woman-haters before, but I could not believe until I saw him actually with my own eyes —simply a miracle to my eyes!

Jennings was rather miserable young fellow, but most kind-hearted. He was a great help to me when I succumbed into penniless poverty a little later on.

I think I attended the Goldsmith Institute about two years, of course with many intervals absence, as usual through financial difficulties.

MY LIFE IN NEW CROSS

The naval office was busy at the time, so that when I came to the class-room I was quite worn-out and unfit to study. The teachers often said to me: "Whatever are you doing with your drawing to-night? You are spoiling all those best parts you have done last night. You look too tired; you had better go back, and go to bed immediately."

But I was too sad to leave my dear class-room before the time. I used to sit down on a chair and smoke cigarettes and watch the others working. I don't know whether I am right or not to mention here about my smoking. It seemed to me, afterwards, that smoking was prohibited in the class-room, although the teachers did not say anything to me. I know I was much spoilt there.

The office was getting still busier. The other secretary was often detained until late at night. I told the attaché that I felt it was not right of me to leave the office while they were all still working. He smiled and said: "Never mind us at all. If you were here for work only, I could get a better worker. I only keep you here for your own sake to study art, so if you feel too tired at the school, I shall let you leave still earlier." And he did that to me!

Captain (now Admiral) Mukoyama, the Naval

attaché, and my great idol, was summoned back to Japan at last. It was the saddest news to me. My Japanese friend Shirasu (the Chancellor of our Legation at the time) came to my room one evening and said to me: " You know Captain Mukoyama is going back to Japan in a few days. I saw him last night, and we talked a great deal about you. He is very fond of you. He has a great confidence in you. I am sure the other officers will be kind to keep you all the same, but remember, our shipbuilding will be quite finished soon, and you will not be wanted any longer. Why don't you go back to Japan soon, if not with the Captain? He might easily push you up through his influence in Japan, and you might have a comfortable life there for all the rest of your days."

Oh, nothing but " comfortable life! " That was not my chief ambition then ! I worried all night. Indeed, this was the first dark cloud in sight, but it was getting bigger and bigger, and later on I met with some of the strongest tempests in my life.

Yes, I worried, but I had already chosen my path—to reject the " comfortable life." In that one sleepless night my nature became absolutely changed from childish gaiety to gloomy misery. From that moment I did

MY LIFE IN NEW CROSS

not laugh heartily for eight long years. If I did laugh or smile at all, it was only to conceal my misery from the public.

Captain Mukoyama called me to his private room at St. James's Place on the day before he left. He said to me: " Now our last day has come; you have been so good to me, I shall miss you very much." Why, I have done nothing for him; it was he who has been so good and so kind to me. How could I pretend myself to accept his words? I was so much moved in tears, and I could hardly lift up my face to see him.

He continued : " I hear you have decided to stay in London. I suppose you are preparing yourself to meet all sorts of difficulties; remember there are some ten thousand artists who are struggling in London. It is not easy matter to live on Art; besides, there are more wolves than sheep wherever you go in this world."

"Yes, my dear Captain, I know it is not easy thing for me. I believe it is not only artists, but engineers, doctors, musicians, and everybody, have enough competitors to struggle against. If one is afraid of his competitors, he cannot succeed in anything at all. I am no cleverer than ordinary peoples, but I have self-confidence to conquer all the difficulties

A JAPANESE ARTIST IN LONDON

by working harder than the others. If they do once, I shall do the same twice, and if they do ten times, I shall do the same a hundred times. It was my ambition from the very first to be quite independent with my art. Only you have been so kind to assist me, but now I feel so courageous to go on with my own way."

"Well said, Markino. One who has the ambition to conquer the world must be so. I believe you shall succeed one day with your own eagerness. However, I know your nature quite well, and I am so anxious to think how much more you shall suffer than those hard-hearted peoples. This world is not so sincere and so neat as you are imagining; but never mind, whenever you meet any difficulty, let me know, I shall assist you all I can."

I think it is no wonder our Navy always wins whenever we have battles. All the sailors would be willing to fight their best under such kind-hearted officers. I myself thought I would fight to death, if I were a sailor under his command.

The next evening I told my teachers and all my class-mates what I was intending to do. Every one of them turned such an anxious face to me. They all said how hard it was to live on Art in London. They looked more

MY LIFE IN NEW CROSS

nervous than I myself felt. Surely they anticipated my future fate more accurately than myself, because they were all English, and they knew English life quite well. I always say, ignorance is the best medicine for timidness. When I crossed the Atlantic Ocean from New York to Havre on board *La Touraine*, we met a strong gale in the English Channel. Big waves washed the deck constantly, and the ship did not move on well. I did not know we were in danger, for I could not understand French. All the passengers and crew seemed very anxious, but I alone was amused with the grand view of the high sea. I was so frightened when I learned afterwards that it was rather a dangerous voyage, and that I might not have lived!

My life voyage was as dangerous as *La Touraine*, only I started with blank ignorance. Mr. Marriott asked me, " Can you draw crowds of people in the streets ? " I said, " No."

" Can you do designs ? "

" No."

" Do you know anything of Architecture ? "

" Not at all."

He was quite pale! I never forget his kind sympathy which so naturally appeared on his face. He said : " You go downstairs to our library and see all those monthly or weekly magazines. You must try to do something like those illustrations."

So I did as he told me and bought some sketch-books, and started studying "figures" at the stations, at the restaurants, at the theatres, and everywhere I went.

At this time I had another secretary friend at our office, and we two used to go together to an A.B.C. for luncheon. I always took out my sketch-book and studied the people. My friend was awfully disgusted with me, and said, "Look at the people, they all are watching you. I am ashamed to come to this restaurant with you. Can't you give up your horrid sketching?"

I said, "By no means could I give up my Art study. If you object to me sketching, let us go to different restaurants quite separately."

When I had luck to spare a few shillings, I often went to a better-class restaurant, not for the luxury of dishes, but to study better-class people.

Oh, I must not forget to mention one thing, of a most faithful waitress at a restaurant in Baker Street. After my meal I left three coppers on the table and went away. When I walked about a hundred yards a policeman stopped me and pointed out for me to look

MY LIFE IN NEW CROSS

back. I saw the waitress chasing after me. She found out a ten-shilling piece between those coppers, so she wanted "to return gold to you." I was much appreciative with her faithfulness. I said, "Really, you had a full privilege to put 'gold' in your pocket. Let us divide this half and half." So I gave her five shillings in spite of my very poverty. She seemed quite happy.

Here in this book I am giving some of those sketches which I did in restaurants at that time. I also began to study drawings from memory. Every night when I came back to my room I used to recollect what I had seen during the daytime and try to draw them from memory. Naturally all the negatives in my head were nothing but young ladies!

It was most surprising thing how little memory I had! Sometimes I remembered only the dress, but forgot all about the hat. Sometimes I caught dress and hat, but forgot the boots. Generally I did their backs, because I had more chance to look at them from the back for a longer time. Here I reproduce some of those studies just to amuse the readers with my struggles on the difficulty.

I was not discouraged with my bad memory. When I was in San Francisco I used to go to fifteen cents meal at some German restaurant. I was quite surprised that those German waiters took more than twelve different orders at one time from us hungry eaters. They never made mistakes. I asked one of them how could he remember all the orders. He said it was only "experience." First time when he became a waiter he took one order, then later on two, three, five, eight, and so on. Indeed, everything is through "experience." So I had patience to get experience some day. I was quite right. After nine years' experience now I can remember a whole crowd of some eighteen or twenty people.

But at the starting-time it was such a difficult task for me. Whenever I went out to the streets I was like a crazy man. More than once I knocked my head against the lamp-posts while I was walking uncautiously, being so busy to study the movement of peoples. The movement of horses was still more difficult to study. Once I ran after a cab in Victoria Street and knocked down a poor little baby. I had trouble with his mother.

How lucky I was that there were no motors in those days, or I might easily have been killed by them!

I had a young lady friend in Lewisham High Road. She wanted me to go to St. John's Church every Sunday evening. Of

MY LIFE IN NEW CROSS

course I could not understand the English enough to enjoy the sermons. It was such a trying hour of waste time there. But at last I got a happy idea. I thought I should study the peoples in the church. I had a Bible with large leather covers. I tore off all the script and put my sketching-book inside the leather cover. In the church I started to sketch during the sermon. My lady friend noticed that one day. She was so shocked. She never asked me to go to the church. Not only that, but our friendship was ended through my vulgar manners. I was sorry to make such savage disturbance on the national religion of England.

She was always very good to explain to me about the ladies' fashions. When I got her last letter, to " end friendship," I rather missed her. Art or Heart? Art or Heart? Both sound so much the same to each other. Cockneys or French peoples might easily mix them up. But to me, there was a great different meaning, and I decided to take Art.

Although my idolised Captain Mukoyama had left the office, the Fleet Paymaster, Mr. Sakura, was as kind as the Captain to me. Once he gave me nine bottles of *saké* (Japanese wine). I had not tasted *saké* since I came to England, so it was a great treat for me. I used to enjoy one or two glasses every evening, and finished two bottles. But that made me so sleepy, and I could not study well after this drink. It was too bad to be so lazy every night. I thought I might give all the rest to my landlord, but he preferred Scotch. It was a pearl to a pig. Too pity to give away such precious thing which we cannot get by money! So I finished all seven bottles in one night.

One gas-light in my room seemed to me to be three or four. The feet of my desk began to wave like snakes. Everything was whirling. I do not know how I got into bed.

Next morning I had bad headache. I was obliged to wire to the office "Too ill to attend." In the afternoon I got up and had a walk. When I went back to the house the landlady told me she was so frightened when she made my bed, my slippers came out from the sheets, and seven empty bottles were lying about the floor. She hoped the kind officers would never give me *saké* any more!

At this time the office removed again to Nottingham Place, near Regent's Park, so I removed to Kensal Rise. The landlady was rather hard-hearted woman. She often made nasty trick on me. I shall not talk much about her, because she was only the one exception during my thirteen years in London.

One day I received my monthly wages at

MY LIFE IN NEW CROSS

the office—five-pound note and some gold. I got on the top of bus. There was a lady with the latest style hat on. I sat down on the back seat and began to study that hat. The conductor came for the fare. I was so busy, and pulled a penny quickly out of my pocket. I got off the bus at Wigmore Street and walked to Marshall and Snelgrove. A lady came to me and said she was so glad to see me. She was the lady whose hat I was studying from the back. I was so surprised. I wondered if English ladies had some more eyes on their back. How dangerous! She was a very kind lady, and she said that as soon as I left the bus the conductor picked up a five-pound note on my seat, and said that he would take that to the Scotland Yard. "Go to Scotland Yard to-morrow morning and you will get your five pounds." That was her kind advice.

Scotland Yard! What was Scotland Yard? I saw a guide-book, and found out it was near Westminster. I thought it must be something Scotch. All the things I knew of "Scotch" were only whisky and my tweed overcoat! I was so curious to see some more of Scotch. I went there next morning. Why, they were all English! Even now I don't understand why it is "Scotland Yard." However, I got my money back, after paying fifteen per cent.

A JAPANESE ARTIST IN LONDON

As I lived at Kensal Rise, I changed my school to London Central School of Art and Craft. At the same time the paymaster told me I should not be needed at the office. It was February of 1901. He gave me two months' notice, with £30. Mr. Wilson was my new teacher at the school. I told him about my position at the time. He encouraged me very much, saying there was an opening for my future if I did my Japanese style. He introduced me to Mr. Holme of *The Studio*. I took a few sketches there, and Mr. Holme accepted them, but said he could not be able to publish them for some months.

March 31st came, and I said good-bye to the office with that thirty pounds, which the paymaster really meant for the boat's fare to go back to Japan. At this moment I could not worry, because I had been worrying quite enough. I was half delighted to think to make my art as my own master, which had been my ambition for ages.

April Fool Day was the anniversary of my artist life. I think that was why I could not be wise with my art business!

As I could not still draw anything well enough to make a picture, I bought Kodak in most ignorant hope to help my art. It was quite useless. I gave it to the daughter of my

MY LIFE IN NEW CROSS

landlady. I bought a wood figure for forty-two shillings. I thought it might be a help to me. It was quite useless too. Only this two-guinea wood figure became a help to me when I was starving in Brixton later on. One of the lodgers in the same house fetched me two shillings from that, "after great difficulty," and I had four meals from that.

I had spent almost all that thirty pounds for the lodging, as well as for buying some "useful things for my Art business" in three months' time. And when I had become quite conscious that there was no other help for my art than my own hard study, I found out only £2, 10s. were left!

My lodging-house was unusually expensive (thirty-five shillings a week) at the time; I had to move to a small house in Mortimer Street, Kensal Rise. Every penny was so precious for me then, so I could not hire a cab for removal. Late at night I tied up all my things. My bag was broken, and I could not use it. So I wrapped everything in my bed quilt, and carried it on my back, and walked to my new diggings some three or four streets. The peoples on the streets stared at me. Perhaps they thought I was a smuggler!

I found this house by a "let" card on the window.

CHAPTER IV

MY LIFE IN KENSAL RISE

THE landlord of my new diggings in Mortimer Street was a blacksmith. He used to go somewhere near Edgware Road to work every day. He told me it was the hardest work in the world, especially in hot summer days, to beat red-hot irons with such heavy hammers near a furnace all day long. I could not lift up his hammer, it was so heavy. I could not believe he lifted it thousands and thousands of times every day.

His wife used to call him "Ted," so I called him "Ted" too. I have forgotten his family name. He married his own cousin, and had three girls and one boy. The eldest daughter was about nine or ten, and the youngest about two years and a half. The latter's name was Clarie, and she was my favourite.

They had such a sweet home, if poor. Many rich peoples ought to be ashamed before them if they saw such a sweet harmony in their devotion to each other. I engaged a very

MY LIFE IN KENSAL RISE

small room in this house for 3s. 6d. a week. They gave me a large kitchen table for my work. When they put this table into my room there was no space to put a single chair, so I used to sit on my bed to work. They charged so little for my meals; practically it was only the original price of the food. I am sure they could not make any profit from my meals.

As I said before, £2, 10s. was all the money I had. Naturally I could not attend to the school any longer; but my teacher, Mr. Wilson, was so kind to call me to his house at Vicarage Gate once a week. He did try all he could to help me. With his introduction letters in my pocket, I used to visit many peoples. Everywhere I was rejected. My £2, 10s. was almost gone. Mr. Wilson himself bought a few drawings of mine for 10s. 6d. each, "just for encouragement." About these drawings I have a strange story to tell the reader.

One evening on July last year (1909), I had a walk on Chelsea Embankment and saw a young Japanese. Naturally I stopped and began to talk with my country-fellow. He said he came to England to study Art, and now he was a pupil of Mr. Wilson's. When this Japanese Art-student met with Mr. Wilson the first time, the latter asked the former if he

A JAPANESE ARTIST IN LONDON

knew a Japanese artist called Yoshio Markino, who lately illustrated the books "The Colour of London" and "The Colour of Paris." The Japanese student said, "No." Then Mr. Wilson brought him my drawings which he bought from me, and said to him, "Look! these were Markino's works about seven years ago. How wonderful that one could get on so well by his own earnestness! I give these drawings to you now. Keep them, and look at them whenever you yourself feel disheartened. They will encourage you."

Then Mr. Wilson told him how he was delighted to hear my "success" (I myself cannot sincerely accept this word just yet, though), and added, "Perhaps Yoshio Markino might be too proud to see me now."

I told my Japanese friend that it was on the contrary. I should be far more delighted to meet my kindest teacher. Only I had been so busy and had no chance. Perhaps I shall see him some day soon.

At Mortimer Street I used to get up at 4.30 or 5.30 in the summer-time, and make all sorts of designs and sketches "for sale," until 9.30, the time of breakfast. Then I had to take them down to the City to show to publishers. Sometimes they would say the managers would like to see me at five o'clock;

MY LIFE IN KENSAL RISE

then, with some bright encouragement, I walked all way back from City to Kensal Rise for luncheon, and walked the same way to the City again, only to meet disappointment, as the managers did not like my work. I used to look at those posters on the dead walls to find out printers' names, then went to the free library to find out their addresses in the post guide. I had heaps of their names and addresses on the back of my sketch-book. I tried every one of them, but all were fruitless. My last penny was gone then, and I got into debt with that poor landlord. His wages were only £2 a week, and he had to keep his wife and four children. I was too sorry for them to take meals there, so I did not come back for luncheons; I used to drink water from fountains in the streets. It was my only luncheon then; my landlady knew that. Every morning when I left the house she used to say to me, "Come back for meals, and please don't starve yourself!"

How could I accept these kind words from such a poor woman? It was only heartbreaking to me; and she also said to me, "Good luck to-day," every morning, and she was waiting me in the evenings to hear "happy news." It was awfully difficult for me to enter into the house after fruitless tasks all

A JAPANESE ARTIST IN LONDON

day, because she was such a sympathetic woman, and she often showed me her tears and said, "Never mind about your debts to us, but I am so sorry for your own hard life!"

So often I wanted some good news, more for her sake than for my own, just to see a smiling face of this kind-hearted woman. Nevertheless, things were still going on harder and harder upon me.

As I walked a good deal every day, my boots were quite worn-out, and my torn-out socks were peeping out almost half the size of my feet. Wherever I went, the editors used to stare at my boots first, then at my works afterwards, with this simple word—"No, thanks."

If I could not come back at the dinner-time I was too sorry to trouble that poor woman, so I used to tell all sorts of lies, that I had a nice dinner out; and many a night I went to bed with my hungry stomach. Indeed, I was too hungry to sleep. A cup of coffee and a few pieces of bread at breakfast were not enough to keep me all day.

When one gets too hungry one's nerves always get sharper. My head was too clear to sleep. I tried not to move quickly, as that made me still more hungry. I lit the gas and began to study anatomy and perspective books. That was the way to avoid waste time in vain.

MY LIFE IN KENSAL RISE

On Sundays I stayed at home all day, and had full meals, and worked out my designs and sketches. My landlord "Ted" used to bring tea and pastries into my room, and say: "Mr. Markino, please take this tea, as a pleasure to me. I cannot bear to see you working so hard without tea." And "Ted" used to offer me one cigarette every night; and he always said, "Smoker has sympathy with smoker." Indeed, it was such a treat for me.

The landlord and his wife both were always as kind as kind could be. They always said to me, "We have never seen a man so honest and so diligent. God bless you. Believe us, you will be all right some day soon." They never pressed me about my debts. They had a little wooden box in which they used to save a few shillings every week for their quarterly "rents." The wife told me they had never touched that money before, as they must be honest and pay their landlord. But now, as I was going to get a few pounds as the copyright from *The Studio* some day, she began to violate her own law, and used to take out sixpence for my luncheons whenever I went out to the City. She said, "It is too great a temptation for me to control. I cannot bear to see such an honest man like you starve."

A JAPANESE ARTIST IN LONDON

While I was thus struggling at Kensal Rise, my old class-mate Jennings got a "better job" (£2, 10s. a week, I believe it was). He wrote me that I should not work so hard all through the week, or else I might get illness. He persuaded me to spend every Saturday afternoon with him. I used to meet him at Westminster Bridge. Then he would take me to Kew, Richmond, Hampton Court, &c. &c., paying all my expenses. He also gave me one pair of his old boots, as mine were too old to wear. Oh, I forgot to mention that I had only two broken socks at this time. I used to wash one pair in my wash-stand every morning before I went out.

At this moment there was only one job for me to get a little money by. It was to be a model at my old school, Goldsmith Institute, at New Cross. Mr. Marriott suggested it to me, and I was delighted to take this job. I had to go there from 2 P.M. until 5 every day. I used to get half-a-crown a day.

My landlord and his wife were so pleased.

I had to take trams on the way there in order to reach there by the time. But on the way back home I walked all the way from New Cross to Kensal Rise in order to give every penny to my landlady. I used to eat my dinner at Lockhart's in Westminster Bridge. Steak and

MY LIFE IN KENSAL RISE

fried onion, sixpence a dish, was a great dinner for me then.

I found out it was not quite easy task to be a model. I was in Japanese costume, and had to sit down like Japanese too. My neck muscles began to crack, and my arm felt as if it was going to be broken. And such a pin and needles! I could not walk for quarter hour after the posing. I did the same thing for three weeks.

Then my pocket began to be dead silent again. How much I envied those who had any sort of work to make livelihood. Even the domestic servants were my great envy! How often I wished to wash windows to get $2\frac{1}{2}$d. each.

A most spoilt child of the Samurai, and a boy-king in his village once, now become a starving unemployee! And I myself was surprised that my heart was become the same as those miserable unemployees too. Indeed, I had such a dirty beggar's heart then. It was one of these days that I saw a gentleman in the Park. He was smoking a cigarette, and he threw away more than half of that unfinished cigarette. I said to myself, "What an extravagant man he is! If he knew what poor life meant, he ought not to do that. It is most cruel thing of him to do that before me!" I

A JAPANESE ARTIST IN LONDON

dared not pick it up, but practically my heart felt just same as if I picked it up. I could not help without recollecting an unfortunate Englishman whom I had met before.

While I was at the Japanese Naval office in Nottingham Place, I often went with my Japanese friends to a billiard-room upstairs of some publican's near by. My Japanese friends went to play billiard, and I to study sketching their movement. There was an old man who was the counter of billiard. We used to give him sixpence, and he was always so grateful to us. One evening while my friends were playing billiard, I had a chat with him. He told me he was once "a very rich gentleman, in an elegant house with stables." He also told me all his sad history, how he was bankrupted. As he was a great sportsman when he was rich, he found out the billiard counter was only the business left for him at last. I asked him, "If you were so rich then, I suppose you often rebel against yourself. Don't you feel it is rather ridiculous that you should thank so politely for our little sixpence? I hope you would not feel that we are insulting you?"

He looked at me with such a happy face, and said, "No, sir; not at all, sir. Sixpence is something so valuable to me, sir." Then he shook my hand, and said in low voice, "This world

MY LIFE IN KENSAL RISE

don't think as you do, sir; you are very kind, sir." I saw his eyes were quite moisted.

Who knows! The time had come that I myself wanted to say, "Sixpence is something so valuable for me!" Indeed, I wanted any work to earn sixpence then. But only one thing was, I could not ask any disgraceful money like chips or charity. Even in my hardest time, it seemed to me the Samurai spirit of my dead father above was always demanding me, "Keep your own dignity."

It was almost useless to try those printing firms any longer. The porters of some firms began to turn most unpleasant faces to me, saying, "You again!" And some of them absolutely refused to let me see the managers. I began to think some other way to earn livelihood. I remembered my old schoolmate Jennings used to work at a tombstone-maker at Norwood, and lately he had left there to get a "better job." It came to mind, "Try that tombstone-maker." But Jennings was having his holidays in Belgium.

I saw the manager of that tombstone-maker only once when Jennings was there. I remembered his name—Mr. Edward—so I wanted to write him. I borrowed twopence again from my landlady. One penny for notepaper and envelope, and the other penny for the postal

A JAPANESE ARTIST IN LONDON

stamp. The very next morning I got a telegram from Mr. Edward—"Come immediately."

My landlady was more pleased than myself. She lent me the traffic fares, and I arrived at Mr. Edward's office on midday. He said he would keep me for thirty shillings a week, and advanced me ten shillings. He told me Jennings was living very cheap somewhere near there, and surely he would be pleased to share his room with me. But unfortunately he wouldn't be back within ten days. So I decided to travel from Kensal Rise during next ten days. All the family at Kensal Rise were so pleased with " good news." I gave nine shillings to my landlady, notwithstanding she refused several times to accept " so much."

She used to make sandwiches every night for my next day's luncheon, and I left there in early morning and walked to Westminster, took the tram to Brixton, and walked the rest. I could not reach to the office before ten. But Mr. Edward " understood " my late arrival. Then, on my back journey, I walked all way from Norwood to Kensal Rise for ten days. It was always quite midnight before I got home. After I removed to West Dulwich I used to send " Ted " ten shillings a week. Alas ! the rent day had come, and my pictures

MY LIFE IN KENSAL RISE

were not published by *The Studio* yet! My poor landlady had trouble with her landlord. It was all through me. It gave me such a pain. I wrote her to mention my name and tell him all the circumstances. To my relief I got her answer—" Don't worry, it is all right; my landlord will wait."

The next month *The Studio* published my sketches, and I was paid all my copyright. I returned all my debts to that most kindhearted landlady in Kensal Rise.

Later on, when I got a little better off, I sent "something" to them, and they were delighted. Last year (1909) I went to Kensal Rise in hope to see these most sympathetic peoples. To my great disappointment everything was changed there, and I could not trace anything of them after eight long years!

CHAPTER V

AT THE TOMBSTONE-MAKER'S IN NORWOOD

THE tombstone-maker's office was situated in front of Norwood Cemetery. It had a little gate, and the building was about a hundred yards back from the street. Many granite crosses and marble angels were exposed in this space. A few fir-trees were growing high up from between those tombstones, the branches of those trees covering the roof of the building. It had a large background, too, where two or three stone-cutters were working from early morning until late evening.

My working room faced to this backyard, and I used to work there quite alone. The first few days I had only to trace some architectural drawings which Mr. Edward had made, then he used to give me some plain drawings of crosses, and other sorts of designs for graves, and which I had to " set in perspective." There were many Scotch and Irish crosses. I often made mistakes with those net-like designs, but Mr. Edward always forgave me.

THE TOMBSTONE-MAKER'S IN NORWOOD

There were so many pathetic inscriptions on those tombstones—" My most devoted wife who passed by so & so," or " My beloved only son died so & so." Here I noticed one thing to prove my philosophy. I found out that there were so many inscriptions which showed that when one of those old couples dies, the other half always dies after a short period. I always had this idea, that when young peoples marry they are in a great love for the first few years, then they begin to quarrel. But when they both pass to fifty-five or sixty years old they become most devoted companions to each other again. If any one doubt this, look at those pathetic inscriptions on the tombstones. One cannot live without the other half in earliest period of marriage, nor in the latest periods. But in the middle ages, it seems to me they are not so broken-hearted: perhaps they become quite jolly widows or widowers. Let us hope to die either quite young or quite old ! I mean, at the happiest moment.

Hitherto I used to have such a bad habit of either whistling or humming some songs while I was working. But in this tombstone-maker's room I began to be quite silent at work. Everything there was too pathetic, and I was in a very serious mood. It was all dead silent. Only those stone-cutters' hammers broke the

A JAPANESE ARTIST IN LONDON

silence with their cling-clang! Occasionally they brought a clumsy wooden waggon to carry away those finished tombstones. The yard was very soft earth and it was quite muddy after the rain, and the wheels were buried deeply into the mud. They had some old wooden planks here and there as " bridges." Men would shout " Ready ? " and the waggon went on with " All right ! " Then such a loud cracking noise ! The bridges were broken, and the waggon sank into the mud a foot deep ! The waggon-horse seemed much annoyed. He shook his head, biting white foam in his mouth. It seemed to me such hard work for him.

At the front office room customers came every day. Generally they were women in mourning. They used to tell the manager all their sad stories—how their husbands were good and kind to them, and how suddenly they got a fatal illness, and how doctors gave up hope; and that their last words were so sweet.

In the case that the customers were too poor the manager used to make " easy terms " for them. Oh, their low and sad voices ! As it was so quiet there every single word of them reached to my ears so distinctly, and I often sobbed in my room.

A blackbird used to come to those trees and sing. Its voice was as sweet as that one which

THE TOMBSTONE-MAKER'S IN NORWOOD

I used to listen to in Greenwich, but how differently it sounded to me! In Greenwich it was a wooing voice, and here it was the voice of the last prayer. Who knows if it was the very same bird! When one's circumstances change, one's feeling changes too.

My diggings at this time were No. 1 Martell Road, West Dulwich, just the other side of Norwood Cemetery. The owners of the house were an old couple with two daughters and one son. The old man was a job worker, and one daughter was telegraph girl. They were very simple and good-hearted, if rough. The old wife had rather quick temper, but was undoubtedly very sympathetic woman. It is true what an ancient Chinese philosopher said, "One who easily gets angry I trust thoroughly; one who always laughs I dread!" I trusted this poor old woman quite heartily, though she often wanted to fight with me. She was always fair in her business matters. I could not believe she knew the word "cheat."

I had a small room just next to Jennings on the top floor, only 14s. including full board a week! Every evening Jennings and I worked together. He used to suggest me some ideas of designs which were "most acceptable to the English publishers." Some evenings we spent all the time looking at illustrated magazines

A JAPANESE ARTIST IN LONDON

and books. We used to buy Pictorial Comedies "between us," and we admired Dana Gibson very much.

On Sunday we often had walk in Dulwich village and Streatham, and it was our "luxury" to buy a box of Sweet Caporal or Ogden's Cigarettes—2½ a box! Ogden's had a portrait of famous English actresses in each package, and I used to collect them. It was the very beginning of my real appreciation of English beauties. Truly I began to admire English beauties too much, and it spoilt my business.

One day Mr. Edward came to me, and said, "Don't you know, Markino, that angel is masculine! For goodness' sake, don't draw such big pectorals on his figure!"

A little later on, he came again and said, "Markino, I am sorry for you, but you see my customers are complaining that your angels look more like ballet girls. I honestly think for your own sake that if you paint real ballet girls you may make more money. I shan't throw you away immediately, so you can come to my office two weeks more. During this time try some publishers with your 'English beauties.'"

When I told this news to Jennings in the evening he said, "I told you so, you naughty boy. You know Mr. Edward is a very religious man. What will you do now?"

THE TOMBSTONE-MAKER'S IN NORWOOD

I said, " I was born so wicked, I would rather give up the 'religious subject' and go into 'English beauties.'"

Thus I lost my permanent situation after three months easy life.

Now my hard life began again. The winter had come. It was the severest winter I ever experienced in London. I remember peoples used to skate on all those lakes in the parks. I could not afford to have fires. Every morning my window had such beautiful web-like designs with ice which did not melt all day long. My hand was too cold to hold my brush. I often went into bed for a few minutes to warm myself. One day I went into a Free Library near my place. I found out it was so warm there, so I used to carry my paper and pencil there and worked there, and if the porter came I hid my sketches under some magazine, as if I were reading the magazine.

The evenings were awfully comfortable because Jennings was at home, and I worked by fire-side in his room, so most parts of my work were done in the night.

One day my landlady brought me a little album and told me her friend wanted me to paint something in it. She said, "I remind you, Mr. Markino, this album belongs to a very religious lady; please don't paint anything too saucy!"

A JAPANESE ARTIST IN LONDON

Alas, I had already begun to be known as "a Saucy little Jap!" I was thinking all night to choose a subject to paint. At last a most "religious" idea came into my mind—a young widow offering flowers to her husband's grave!

Strange to say, after some seven years, when I had become acquainted with the peoples at my publisher (1908), one of the clerks came to me and said, "Mr. Markino, do you remember you painted a picture in the album which belonged to my sister-in-law in Norwood?"

Once or twice in a week I used to come out to the City with my designs. This time I was a little luckier. Sometimes those lithograph companies bought some "effective" designs for a guinea each. But I had unsuccessful journey oftener. Some managers said my pictures were too Japanese, while the others said they were too European. There was a comical story about it. One day I was in a great hurry to wrap up my pictures, and by mistake I took one of Jennings' works together. A manager looked so unpleasant with my works because they were "too Japanese." He picked up that picture by Jennings and said, "Look here, it is too Japanese. English publics would not understand such design." I said very politely, "Pardon me, but it is done by my English friend." He was rather perplexed. "Oh, I

THE TOMBSTONE-MAKER'S IN NORWOOD

am afraid your friend is too much influenced by you!"

My friend told me not to take too seriously all what they said. It was only their excuse. If they really like my work they would take it whether it was "too Japanese" or "too English."

One publisher gave me a commission to do a book of some two dozen small designs for twelve guineas. I finished them in a week. I was looking forward for the immediate payment. No cheque came day after day. I had only half-penny then. I found out some very very old pictorial postcard in the bottom of drawer, so I wrote on the card asking the immediate payment. Next day I got a letter from them. Twelve guinea cheque was in it, but they expressed their anger because I wrote on a postcard, and added that I must not be so ignorant of the publisher's customs—the payment on publication. Jennings told me they were only too kind. They might easily bring a libel action against me using postcard for money matters.

I was so frightened—a quite new lesson about English custom once more! I wrote an apologising letter to them.

However, Jennings and I were quite happy. He called me "a rich man." We both decided

A JAPANESE ARTIST IN LONDON

to remove to Brixton, because it was so inconvenient for both of us to live so far away from the City. I spent several days for hunting a new digging in Brixton district.

It was this time that the Anglo-Japanese Alliance was announced. When I was passing that large space near Brixton Station several English sailors surrounded me. Evidently they must have been on Japanese water some time for their duty. They began to squeeze out from their head all Japanese words they remembered. As soon as they saw me they shouted, " Banzai ! " " Ohayo," or " Konnichiwa." One of them started to talk to me, and his beginning word was " Sayonara " (" Good-bye "). I was much amused with their childish innocence. They carried me to a " Pub " near by and had a drink for our Alliances. I whispered a few words which they might probably have heard from tea-house girls. My anticipation was quite right. They were so delighted, and laughed.

Now, leaving the question of the Anglo-Japanese Alliance aside just for a while, Jennings and I, a private Anglo-Japanese Alliance, found out our diggings at No. 151 Brixton Road.

CONSTITUTION ARCH

AUTUMN

REGENT'S PARK

LIFE CLASS

EARL'S COURT STATION

OUTSIDE ST GEORGE'S HOSPITAL.

HYDE PARK CORNER

THE THAMES AT RANELAGH

CHAPTER VI

MY LIFE IN BRIXTON

Our Anglo-Japanese home at 151 Brixton Road was an ordinary boarding house occupied by an old couple and one step-daughter. Jennings and I engaged one bed-room and one sitting-room, where I used to work all day. About ten or eleven lodgers were staying. Most of them were students for chemists, and commercial travellers. There was one law student called Bevan, a quite young and bright fellow, with much ability. Lately I heard he is getting on splendidly as a solicitor somewhere about Tottenham. He and I became great friend, and I used to call him " Scientific Liar," and he called me " Mock British Lion."

It was this time Mr. Grant Richard published my " Little Japanese Dumpy Book." The weekly magazine *King* took several sketches of mine. But luck did not smile upon me regularly. One day Jennings and I noticed that the landlady "turned out" one lodger because he could not pay regularly.

A JAPANESE ARTIST IN LONDON

We looked at each other's eyes rather seriously. Jennings said, "Never mind, if you could not pay I shall pay that for you." I think he did so for a few weeks. Sometimes publishers accepted my works but never published. More seldom my pictures were published, but not paid. Bevan told me that I ought to make the contract each time. "In England," he said, "it is the only way. And if it is in black and white it is quite safe." But whenever I saw a new person he looked to me so gentle and so kind-hearted, and every time I thought, "Oh no, this gentleman would never cheat me," and I worked without contract, only to repent afterwards. Bevan thought I was most "hopeless, foolish fellow for business" he has ever seen.

I got into a heavy debt with the landlady again. I was so frightened that she might turn me out every minute. But to my surprise (and delight, too) she said to me, "Oh no, we shan't turn you out; your case is quite different from the other. I know those wealthy peoples never pay you properly, but never mind, we shall always feed you well." Unfortunately this kind-hearted old woman died in a few months, and the peoples of this house asked all the lodgers to have meals out until they were quite settled down. I under-

MY LIFE IN BRIXTON

stood they were almost broken-hearted and could not manage our meals every day. Jennings felt so inconvenienced about that, and he removed some other house, but I myself was quite penniless and had some debts, so I could not remove. I took only one small bedroom on the top floor. A chemist student, one of the lodgers, was very kind to me. He used to take my pictures to the City, and sold one or two for me. It was this time he sold my wooden figure for me too.

But that was not enough, and I began to be a hermit again. Day after day I had to go to bed without any meal. This time I got a little bad impression with some English business peoples, because if they only were honest enough to pay me what they promised I need not suffer this starvation. Indeed I had far more credit than my actual debts. I still keep my diary of this time. On one of its pages I find this passage: ". . . did not send me the cheque to-day again. What dirty commercial spirits they have in their heads! Money to these people is just like fishes to cats. I do hate these merchant spirits. It doesn't matter to me, after all, whether I get two pounds or twenty pounds. If I get more I only spend more to please other peoples. Money does not affect me enough to hate

A JAPANESE ARTIST IN LONDON

this world, but just imagine those dirty merchant spirits! This dirty feeling perishes all good friendship. I suppose everywhere in this world is just same. So I have not much hope to live in this world now. Damn the dirty wicked world! What use to live in such a place—Devil's Den! I am not very hard on individuality, because it is their own weakness after all. But how pity they can not cure their most incurable hereditary illness!"

But another page of this diary says, " Went to the National Gallery and spent a whole morning there. I saw many peoples inside. They all were so humble before those old masterpieces. Who knows if they were same sorts of peoples with those who are treating me worse than their dogs. Perhaps they themselves might be those dirty commercial peoples. But in front of the masterpieces they behave themselves so nicely. Very well then, very well! I shall make a 'masterpiece' some day and let all those dirty commercials kneel down in front of me! It is all through my faults that I should be treated like this now because my Art is not good enough *now*. But some day, yes, some day. . . ."

At this very moment I got a letter from my elder sister in Japan. She is thirteen years older than myself and I was her pet at home.

MY LIFE IN BRIXTON

In her letter, she expressed that she began to feel that her young age was nearly gone by, and she was so lonely that she was thinking of me more than ever. She dreaded to be awake with her dream at midnight that I was dead; and she wished so much to see me just once more, because when I ran away to America from Tokio, I did not go back home to say good-bye to her. "And," she continued, "if it is impossible for you to come back now, please let me hear some bright news, and don't forget to send me your photo, too!"

I never wrote her about my hard life, as I was afraid it would upset her. But she began to be alarmed with my long silence. Her letter was only a dagger to my heart. How fortunate that my sister did not see me borrowing 2½d. from my English friend for the post stamp which I put on my answering letter.

My answer to her was quite simple—a Japanese poetry in four lines:—

"The lofty summit of the mountain is almost in sight,
But the road around the precipice is too much curved.
You must, I understand, be tired of waiting a long, long age,
Though I, myself, am climbing incessantly all this time, without rest."

I was then such an ambitious boy, and I wanted "name" in vain. I used to write all what I felt in my note-book. It says, "London is such a large town. It is really too large. Something like a big ship. I cannot move it with my strength." I remember when I was a boy I went to a sea shore and saw a large European boat. It was the first time in my life to see such a large ship. I got up to the top of the cabin. I wanted to jump on the deck, but I was afraid I might make such a noise, as I often made in the school-room when I jumped from the desk to the floor, and that I might shake the whole boat, then the Captain would be angry with me. But at last I decided to jump on the deck. Why, such a hard deck! I made no shaking, only I hurted my feet so much.

"Now in London, if I try to make sound with London, London does not sound at all, only I hurt myself. That is all."

It was only just a few weeks ago (Nov. 1909) that I received a most flattering letter from my most intimate friend: "Be courageous, Markino, London had begun to move a little by your brush." Alas, I am grown up and no more a boy slave of "fame." My present ambition is only to improve my art. Any favourable or unfavourable criticisms are no account to me. Only nice subject and nice composition are my real delight.

Well, getting back to my Brixton life. The

MY LIFE IN BRIXTON

King's Coronation Day was coming. Mr. Gordon Home, the editor of *The King*, commissioned me to make four sketches—two naval reviews seen from a Japanese cruiser and two processions in London streets. That meant some twenty pounds—a great fortune for me then! But all my delight was robbed by the King's illness. I had pain as if I myself were operated!

I think I concealed all my misery fairly well before the public. For at my starving time I called on *Harper's Magazine* at Albemarle Street several times. The manager said, "You must be getting on quite prosperous. You look always so happy." How lucky he had no X-ray apparatus to see my empty stomach! He was, anyhow, very kind to introduce me to a French lady artist, who had a studio in Hammersmith. She gave me some jobs to paint some Geisha's portrait on the cloth cover for portfolios. I was paid half-crown each and I could paint two every day. This job continued for a few months, and my diggings began to serve the lodgers full meal, too.

One of these evenings my landlord came into my room and said, "A Japanese gentleman come to see you, sir." I opened my door and I heard voice downstairs: "O-yi Markino! Bokuda, Bokuda!" ("It is I, it is I!")

A JAPANESE ARTIST IN LONDON

I shouted, "Who are you; whose name is 'I'?"

The next second I met him on the middle of stairs. It was my dear Japanese poet friend, Yone Noguchi! He told me he had just arrived from New York to Queen's Hotel in Leicester Square. He removed to my address immediately, and had a room just downstairs of mine.

For the first few nights, naturally, I was so busy to ask him about my friends in Japan as well as in America, then we began to talk each other's experiences since we were parted. He had a little better opinion on America, because he spent most part of his time in Washington and New York, where the Japanese were not so much hated as in California. He used to say English peoples are so slow, and he called me a cow, because my temperament was "so slow" too.

"Markino," he often exclaimed, "you are getting too English altogether." But one day he received a letter from his worshipped friend, Mr. Charles Warren Stoddard. It ran something like this:—

"Yes, my dear Yone, you may think English people are very slow; you may not like them now. But be patient and stay there a little longer. Some day you will find out something

MY LIFE IN BRIXTON

at the bottom of English people's hearts—some gentleness, some sweetness, which other nations seldom have. When you have once recognised this you will never forget it all your life."

Yone was a very sharp observer. It did not take long time that he fell into love with the English peoples. Indeed, after only four months' stay in London when I went to see him off at Paddington Station I saw his eyes were much inflammated with tears. He peeped out from the train window and said to me, " I am sure I shall come back to England. Yes, I must come back again. I promise you faithfully. So you wait here until I come. Markino, you are a lucky fellow to stay in sweet London all the time."

Yone's four-month visit to London was my great comfort. We both had something nobler and sweeter than anything which one can get with money. Although I was meeting great sympathy of those landladies wherever I went, my art was suffering a great deal through their ignorance. Now Yone was my complement. It was this time that he told me the story of Keats, which I wrote in my essay of "The Colour of Rome." Yone used to sit on a chair in front of the fire-place stretching his two feet high above the mantel-piece, drooping his head on his chest and grasping his two hands together

A JAPANESE ARTIST IN LONDON

on his back. Whenever I came back into the room it was my great delight to see this peculiar pose of his.

We two often had walk along the Victoria and Albert Embankment in nights to enjoy London fogs. I remember he made many poetries about London Mists. I wonder if he ever published them. Yone thought the English publishers were "too slow" for the publication of his works, so he decided to publish them himself. We saw the advertisements of those job printers, and found out the one at Kennington was the fairest. Yone ordered him to print some two or three hundred copies of his few poetries on brown paper. It was about sixteen pages, entitled, "From the Eastern Sea," by Yone Noguchi, a Japanese. Price two shillings. A messenger came from that printing-office to see Yone especially about the lettering of the price. He asked Yone again and again to assure that it was really two shillings and not two pence! Yone gave him positive answer. After the messenger was gone Yone told me that the messenger looked into his face so seriously to find out if Yone's head was "a bit off," and we laughed so much until our landlord's dog began to bark at us!

I think it was about the evening of February

MY LIFE IN BRIXTON

13, 1903, Yone and I went to the printing-office, and a few hundred copies of "From the Eastern Sea" was ready, so we carried them home. It was such a cold night and my hands had no feeling at all. Then the pavement was quite frozen, and it was so slippery and almost impossible to walk with my worn-out boots. Yone warned me not throw them on the mud because he could not afford to print them again.

On the same night Yone sent more than half to some important literary people and newspapers. Every one of them welcomed this little brown book (pamphlet, rather), but one of them (I think it was Mr. William Rossetti) wrote Yone kindly enough to warn him that unless he obeyed the regulations of Publishing Law he would be punished. We both were so frightened, and next day we went to Stationers' Hall and registered his name and sent copy each to the British Museum, Oxford, and Cambridge. Many people came to buy Yone's book. About business matter he was as bad as myself. He could not ask the payment. He presented each copy to everybody who came to buy. One evening he said to me, "I cannot afford to present all my book."

I said, "Of course you cannot; why don't you ask them the payment?"

A JAPANESE ARTIST IN LONDON

"But, Markino, just think how could I ask two shillings for this, although I put on that price?"

While we were talking a very young fellow came to buy Yone's book. It was Arthur Ransome (he was only seventeen or eighteen then). I told Ransome that Yone wanted two shillings a copy. Ransome was willing to pay. Yone shouted, "No, Markino. It is 'lie!' it is 'lie!'" and he ran out of the room. However, Ransome insisted to leave two shillings. We decided to buy some cigarettes, and when Ransome came we three should enjoy the smoking. Afterwards I learnt that Ransome was as poor as we were then.

Soon after this the Unicorn Press wanted to publish a more "elaborate" edition, and I made a design for the book-cover—many Japanese boats loaded with parchment sailing forward, and each sail had Yone's family crest. My original design was dark indigo on bluish-grey ground. Yone liked it very much. But to our great disappointment the publishers printed it vermilion on cream ground—to make it more "effective." I said, "Effective? Indeed, it is effective enough to make us sick! Commercial elaboration means our Hell!"

I think Yone made several nice friends here,

MY LIFE IN BRIXTON

in whose heads he is still well remembered for evermore. But he had gone so soon. I not only missed him so much, but began to sink into the financial difficulty again. Perhaps it was worse than ever. My debts for the landlord were getting higher and still higher. I had less courage to try and sell my pictures this time, because it was so difficult to get payment after "accepted," and I could not try same places again.

It was one of these days I was walking near Hyde Park Corner, I felt something on my chest, somebody was striking me with his stick. It was Ukida Goji, a Japanese Chancellor. He said to me, " Here, here, are you still living ? "

I was not clever enough to answer such a difficult question, so I passed on in silence. The day-time I was so busy to try some publisher, but when I went to bed at night I began to recollect those words, " Are you still living ? " I could not understand why should I be so insulted like that, only because I was poor ! My pillow case was quite wet with my tears. Really, I need not take him so seriously, as he was only an insignificant chancellor !

CHAPTER VII

I DECIDE TO COMMIT SUICIDE

WITH such fruitless task day after day I was much discouraged, and moreover I was so disappointed with this false and faithless world. One morning I quite decided to commit suicide, if that day's task were fruitless again. Though I was such a quite worthless little man, and it would make no difference whatever to the world whether I died or lived, it was something for me to die. It could not be a joke to me, I was in such a serious mood. Even now I cannot forget that feeling. Let me write down all my impressions at that moment.

As I am a Japanese I could not believe that suicide was a crime. If there is crime in a suicide case, the crime does not belong to the one who commits suicide, but to those who so cruelly drived suicider into such decision. They deserve the name "manslaughterer," if not "murderer."

I have a most pathetic story, which I want to tell to the English readers. Some years

I DECIDE TO COMMIT SUICIDE

ago there was a most innocent and sacred little girl, like an angel, in Japan. By some misfortune she was captured by some American blackmails. The poor girl found out that she was going to be sold as a prostitute in America. There was no way for this helpless creature to escape her future doom. She committed suicide, leaving a poetry which is even now repeated incessantly by every Japanese mouth. It ran thus:

"Tsuyu wo dani ito-o Yamato no Ominaeshi, furu America in Sode wa nura saji."

"Even a drop of dew is dreaded by a little meadow flower of Japan.
How could she bear to make her sleeves wet amid the pouring rain?"

(*Ame* is *rain* in Japanese language, so she used *America* as *rain* with double meaning.)

Indeed she was too pure to be ruined by those barbarous Americans. The Japanese judge had sense enough not to pass the sentence of "unsounded mind" on her. But we all worship her as the sacred mirror of the highest ethics.

There is always something higher and nobler than our life. That is our human dignity. For this higher and nobler dignity that innocent yet most graceful girl gave up her life.

A JAPANESE ARTIST IN LONDON

Not only for her own dignity, but for the dignity of her country, the daughter of Japan killed herself. But she is immortalised for ever!

We, each individual, have each our own bodies, but our conscience is only one conscience, common to all of us. Therefore it is most selfish to kill the sacred conscience, which is common to others, for the sake to save our own life.

Look at those Early Christians! Thousands of them met their death because they refused to give up their faith.

Of course they did not kill themselves, other peoples did that. But what is the difference—killing themselves by their own hand or by the other people's hands? I call them "suicides" all the same. Jesus Christ Himself knew those Jews would kill Him, yet He gave up Himself to them. It was, in a manner, suicide. Why then do the English judges not condemn Christ? Why do they not call Jesus Christ "unsounded mind"? Of course there are many who are really "unsounded mind."

I myself was not a coward to be afraid to face these difficulties. There was something, which I shall not write here to avoid the trouble of any libel action. But, truly, I

I DECIDE TO COMMIT SUICIDE

hated some faithlessness and I could not sell my dignity for that. Oh, let the judges call me "unsounded mind" if they like. But I would call those faithless fellows "unsounded mind" by return. It is not myself alone I am sure. How many innocent souls in this world are being driven into this state every year—nay, every week, or even every day? The one who drives them this way must have the same crime with the one who pierced the spear into the side of Jesus Christ, or as Judas Iscariot.

Even at this moment I was not absolutely pessimistic with the whole world. How could I forget those pathetic, sweet, English women in those lodgings? Besides, I recollected some little sweet story which my brother told me when I was a boy: "One summer morning, when the dawn came, Miss Morning Glory said, 'I shall blossom when my little Master Dew comes to me!' Little Master Dew said, "I shall go to see Miss Morning Glory when she blossoms!' While they were waiting each other, the cruel hot summer sun came and perished both Miss Morning Glory and Little Master Dew."

In this wide world there are plenty friends in the same opinion, only it is always one's fate that one does not meet with them. My

A JAPANESE ARTIST IN LONDON

Art was my Miss Morning Glory. Surely there must be many Master Dews? But they did not come to me, so my Art was going to be perished by some faithless ones, without blossoming.

But what does it make different to this world whether my Art blossom or not? We all must die some day sooner or later. I could not help without being jealous with those soldiers and sailors. If they die on the battlefield, their names shall be celebrated by the whole nation. If they come back alive, they shall be fully decorated as the triumphers!

It was quite different in my case. If I die, I must die like a dog. If I live, I must meet all insults. And the cruelty in peace time is greater torture than bullets and swords on the battlefield. The hardship on the battlefield is all flowers. The difficulty in peace time is nothing but dust. Oh, why did I not become a soldier or a sailor? I shut my eyes and saw a mental vision. Some dirty deceivers were sneering at me. My sister and brother were weeping besides. My dead mother and father were beckoning me from above the sky in misty clouds, and so vividly I saw all my friends' faces. In the far distance I heard my own voice faintly. It was that poetry

I DECIDE TO COMMIT SUICIDE

I sang at Yokohama wharf just before I sailed:

" When the son of Samurai decides to step out from the threshold,
He would sooner die than come back before his Ambition is fulfilled.
Why should he worry where to bury his bones?
Wherever he goes, there is a green hill."

I opened my eyes and wondered if my expression was changed. I looked at my glass and I found no change. I could show a jolly smile. Ah, that is all right.

I left no note. I was intending to hide my corpse by drowning. I did not want to trouble anybody, neither I wanted the judgment of that ridiculous " temporary insanity." I looked back to my old room again and again, and recollected all my history there.

The first place I tried on this day was *The Magazine of Art*. I have never tried this magazine before because it was such a high art magazine, and I was told that art magazines never pay to artists. But at the time I had such a great question to answer—Death or Life? I got courage to try it.

CHAPTER VIII

THE LOOSENING OF THE ROPE

From Brixton Road to Ludgate Hill every step of my feet made my heart beat. Death or Life—that was my question on each step. The porter of Cassell's took me to a little reception room, where I waited a few minutes. The assistant editor of *The Magazine of Art* (I think it was Mr. Fisher. I am such a bad one to remember English names) came to see me first. He was so polite, and so modest. I felt myself something more like a human at last. We say in Japan, " If you want to see a house master's nature, look at his servants how they behave themselves." It was quite true in this case. He said he would take my portfolio to show to Mr. Spielmann. Perhaps Mr. Spielmann would come out to see me himself if I waited there awhile.

Mr. M. H. Spielmann? I knew his name before, because Yone Noguchi told me he was a great art critic. While I was waiting in the room I already began to feel some great comfort through Mr. Fisher's kind treatment.

THE LOOSENING OF THE ROPE

After some five minutes the great art critic came into the room with my portfolio in his arm. He promised me to buy some of them and publish all my sketches. I myself thought I was such a clever actor to conceal all my anxieties from him. He never told me anything what he saw in me. But after a few years, when he wrote the introduction chapter of "The Colour of London," to my great surprise I found out these words in his writing: "He looked tired and pale. . . . I promised to buy one or two: his eyes danced, &c. &c."

Now I see I was not quite a successful actor. His eyes must be X-ray.

What a sharp observer he was! This has added more confidence of mine on his profession too. I think it is my turn now to write my first impression of him. I hope Mr. Spielmann will forgive me that, because he himself did the same.

By his appearance I thought he must be very sensitive. By his speech with such a great rapidity, yet each syllable pronounced so distinctly, I thought he must be very particular on everything, either publicly or privately. That was not all, but I found out some most sympathetic pitch in his voice which was buried in the bottom so deep that he would not show his kindness much outwardly as most hypocrite would. This was my very first impression on him at a glance. I am always very proud that my judging was not mistaken.

A few days later he asked me to write a sketch of my life-story, and also he wanted me to tell him how much I needed for my work.

So I wrote him a short essay on my life, and said, "As your magazine is devoted for the art, I know it will do me good by your publication. I really must not ask you any remuneration at all. It is only your kindness to speak about any payment, so please do just as you like."

Next morning I found Mr. Spielmann's answer on my breakfast-table. "After reading your most pathetic essay, I cannot take your advantage. Please find the cheque enclosed. . . ."

He bought two pictures with full prices (the best price I ever had before), and also offered me the copyright for the others.

My Morning Glory has met with the tenderest Dews just by the time!

Ever since, for some seven years, Mr. Spielmann has been always Dew to a dying Morning Glory. It will be quite a thick volume if I write out every kindness he has done for me. I have three names for him:—

1. The rescuer of my life.
2. The father of my Art, because he has been

THE LOOSENING OF THE ROPE

doing all sorts of good for my Art from both points of view—study, as well as selling.

3. The Custom House for all my English friends, because it was he who introduced me to all my most valuable friends I have now.

About the same time I met with Mr. Lee Warner. He was the Art Editor of the *English Illustrated Magazine.* His office was in the upstairs of one of those old houses at Paternoster Square. The stairs were worn out in the shape of cow's back. The floor of his room was inclined to one way, so pens or pencils would not stop on the same place where you drop them. The walls were not right angle to each other, either, at the corner. It was something like an architecture painted by a very modern impressionist.

Whenever I went there I always thought, if ever an earthquake were occurred in London, he must be the first person to be buried under the roof.

He accepted some of my work for his magazine and also introduced me to the editors of *Black and White*, where I worked several weeks continually. Mr. Lee Warner, too, was very kind to get many commissions for me. My sketches and articles, accompanied with a note of Mr. Spielmann's, were published in August number of the *Magazine of Art*. Mr. Douglas

Sladen was the very first person who wrote to Mr. Spielmann a letter which I had privilege to look at with a delight. It ran like this:—

". . . This month's number of your magazine is most interesting, especially about that Japanese artist. Will you send him to me; I think I can put him in the way of some work."

From this time I used to illustrate the novels by Mr. Sladen.

Mr. Teignmouth Shore, too, wrote to Mr. Spielmann to send me to him. He was the Editor of the *Academy and Literature* then. I wrote some articles about my impressions of the English stage. I needed a dictionary to write my essays, so I went to a discount stationary and bought "Twentieth Century Dictionary" for 2s. 6d. I hurried to my room with this dictionary in my arms. I was so excited to see inside, I turned all pages from the beginning to the end. I saw so many Japanese words, such as "Banzai," "Kami," "Kakemono," "Tsuba," &c. I was so surprised. Are they already nationalised into English? How quick they are! Surely they have come to England some time after I did. And fancy they were already Anglicised! They are wonderful progressives, and I myself am such a dreadful Conservative! I used to worship this

THE LOOSENING OF THE ROPE

very "progressive" dictionary until Arthur Ransome so kindly gave me a book called "Unspeakable Scotch" by Mr. Crosland! He said, "This is such an interesting book. Everybody laughs to death to read it. Oh, you must read it."

I opened the book and wrestled every word with my worshipped Dictionary. Why, this very Cosmopolitan Dictionary never gave Scotch words! I had to give up reading. How disappointing! Indeed Mr. Crosland's "Unspeakable Scotch" was my only unreadable book then.

One morning a postcard was awaiting me on my breakfast table. It was written in Japanese. "I have finished my three years' study in Germany, and now I have come to London to have a sightseeing before I go back to Japan. But as I cannot speak a single English word I cannot come to your place. Will you come out to Albert Dock to fetch me? I am on board the Japanese steamship *Kawashi* which I took from Antwerp."

It was from Colonel Surgeon Morinami.

Morinami was my brother's most intimate friend, and he used to spoil me when I was a child. I could hardly finish my first cup of coffee, and went to the Albert Dock. A middle-aged Japanese gentleman was walking up and

A JAPANESE ARTIST IN LONDON

down on the wharf. He seemed thinking something seriously and quite absent-minded. . . . He did not answer to my "Good-morning." I asked him if he met with Colonel Morinami on board that ship. He said "I am Morinami." I shook his hand and said "I am Markino."

"Oh, you are Hei-bo?" (My boy-name was Heiji, so I was called Hei-Bo or Little Master Hei.)

Naturally we could not recognise each other, as I saw him last when I was only nine years old!

We began the sightseeing immediately. First of all I took him to the Medical Museum at Lincoln's Inn Fields, as he was a surgeon. Then, in four days' time, we had seen almost all important places. He was amazed with the size of Crystal Palace and the "wonderful" structure of Black Wall Tunnel, the "sacred dignity of old Westminster Abbey and St. Paul," and the thick crowds in the City. But he had more sense than only to be amazed with large buildings or busy metropolitan life. He was especially so keen about educational works. All museums like "British," "South Kensington," &c. &c., were his greatest admiration. When he saw those ship and train models and Natural History Museum at South Kensington he sunk into such a deep thought. He could

THE LOOSENING OF THE ROPE

not answer to my single question—" What do you think of these?"

After such a long silence, he began to open his mouth at last. " In Germany I have never seen such perfect museums. How wonderful is the British Nation about voluntary works for the public education! Just one glance at these museums is worth far more than one year study in Japan. I heartily admire the Britons. I heartily respect the Britons, and I sincerely envy them too."

Every evening after the dinner we talked until one or two A.M. Nothing could be more interesting to me than to hear all the news of my home village. Such a change since I left there, that the wild fields where I used to gather mushrooms are turned into mulberry fields, and some silk manufacturing firms are puffing thick smokes from their chimneys: that hundreds of poor girls are summoned there by a steam whistle every morning: that the manager of an old inn has become a wealthy man and builded a large European-style house; that my old nurse died and her daughter, who was only a few-years-old baby when I left there, is now married, and the road was widened for more frequent traffics, &c. &c.

Then he told me all his experiences at Chino-Japanese War. As he was a surgeon he did

A JAPANESE ARTIST IN LONDON

not go near the actual fighting spots, but those poor wounded soldiers were only the cause of heart-rending to look at.

One day he was mixed up among those defeated Chinese, and suddenly the shower of bullets were poured upon him from a Japanese force. More than twenty Chinese fell dead around him in a few seconds. He was quick enough to pick up a long spear which some Chinese left, and fix a Red Cross flag and wave it. The Japanese trumper signalled "stop fire," and he joined to his regiment again safely. "But," he said, "the battlefield was nothing comparing with my hardest time for studying." And he told me what a hard time he had to study the medical lessons. I told him all my experiences in America and in London. I also told him my opinion about the suicides, which I had decided only a few weeks back.

"Ah, now I see," he exclaimed, "you were not a madman."

"How do you mean by that?" I asked.

"Oh," he exclaimed, rather surprisedly, "I forgot to tell you what I heard of you in Germany." Then he told me that he spoke to all his Japanese friends in Berlin that he was intending to meet me in London. Some Japanese Chancellor said to him: "Yes, there is a

THE LOOSENING OF THE ROPE

Japanese called Yoshio Markino in London. But he is a madman. Don't go to see him." Whereupon Morinami answered him, " Well, let Yoshio be a madman if you like. He is my villager, and I am much indebted with the kindness of his father, Mr. Toshimoto Markino, when I was a boy. I must see Yoshio Markino whatever you say." Thus he came to me. "So you see," he went on, " I am so glad to see you. I can thoroughly imagine why that Chancellor called you a madman. You can imagine that, too!" (I hope the reader can imagine, too.)

" Never mind of him. Not only I alone, but all our nation must be grateful to you that you have not stained even a dot on the dignity of our country all through your hard life. Perhaps you may still meet more hardships again in the future. But always remember you are in a strange country, and the strange nations are always watching you every day. Do not forget a minute that you are representing our country here. As regards your opinion of suicide, I thoroughly agree with you. Do commit suicide if it were necessary for the sake of our high ethic. I, myself, shall have all the responsibility, and I shall fight against the world to prove you were not 'unsounded mind,' but show them your ethical theory and

A JAPANESE ARTIST IN LONDON

Yamato Damashii (the patriotic soul of Japan). But what I sincerely expect is your success. And when you succeed, do come back to your sweet home once more."

"Come back to my sweet home? I have no home now. My family was almost bankrupted and our old home was sold a long time ago. And you said yourself, that everything is quite changed at our village."

"Nay, do not say so! your brother is leading a poor life, but full of honours, and all the villagers are paying their homage to him. Most of those old villagers who used to spoil you are all dead now. But their children never forget you. They are still very loyal to your family; such a loyalty you cannot imagine in Europe. Even the views, though they are changed, you shall find some sweetness in them to recollect your early life. You know that temple Shimmei Sama? I used to spin the tops in front of that sacred stone lantern when I was a child. Now that lantern is removed away except the foundation stone, but whenever I go back there now this very foundation stone always tells me the history of my childhood. Nothing in this world could be sweeter than home. Therefore come back home once more. All your schoolmates are scattered all over Japan now, but I shall gather them all to our Koromo village

THE LOOSENING OF THE ROPE

when you come back, and all the villagers shall have a holiday to welcome you. Whenever the northern wind of England blows too severe against you, just think that warm and mild hearts wait for you at Koromo. If the whole world throw you away, Koromo village alone will always be ready to welcome you most heartily. River Yahagi is clean enough to wash all the worldly dust you get, and Mount Sanage is high enough to prevent the cruel northern wind."

"Ah, the northern wind of England may be too severe and too cruel. But I need it. I think we Japanese rely upon each other too much. Through the severeness and cruelty in my daily life I am learning a great lesson. That is the spirit of Independence. Look at each individual Briton! How independent they are! They are my teachers. The flower of almond blossoms in chilly February, and when the severest northern wind blows it scatters its noblest fragrance all over the world. Let me stay in England until the last leaf of my flowers is blown off. I am contented!"

"Oh, you misunderstood me. I did not mean to persuade you to come home altogether, but remember to pay a visit when you can."

The morning of the fifth day came, and I went to Charing Cross station to see him off.

A JAPANESE ARTIST IN LONDON

We were some twenty minutes too early. We waited the last minutes on the platform. The Colonel Surgeon passed his eyes from my head to my feet. "You are grown-up! You were such a comely, girl-like child, and I used to carry you on my back, you remember?"

The cruel clock hands never stopped. The shrilling steam whistle penetrated into my heart. The porter banged the train door. One hatless Japanese head was hastily thrust out from the window. It was the last sight of Morinami. "Sayonara, Sayonara," and "Sayonara!" Each Sayonara sounded more and more faintly. A thick smoke from the engine veiled his face invisible.

When it was cleared up he and the train were no more in sight. For some minutes I stood on the same platform like a corpse without soul. So absent-minded I was when I walked out the station that I struck myself against a pedlar. I bought a box of matches which I really did not want, and I don't remember how much I paid him. A bus drive from the station to my place took twenty-five minutes. I went into my room and locked my door. Now nobody could see me at last! My self-controlling power was overcome, and I cried like a baby.

To wipe off my tears, I went to Hampstead

THE LOOSENING OF THE ROPE

to see Mrs. Dryhurst in the same evening. I had made an acquaintance with her some time ago. I stopped at her house until twelve. She lent me " Chuchuland " by Lady Gregory. It was quite new book. I took it back with me, and when I came to Blackfriars I got on the last tram. A dirty woman took a seat by side of me and shouted: "'Allo John, won't ye piy ma fare?" I was so frightened that I jumped off from the tram. I fell down quite flat and threw "Chuchuland" some yards away. It was buried in mud! I begged Mrs. Dryhurst to let me buy a new copy for her. But she insisted not to do so. She would keep it as a souvenir of my adventure on that night. This book was awfully interesting, and Irish legends resembled closely with some of Japanese.

Since this time I was a frequent visitor to Mrs. Dryhurst, who introduced me many interesting peoples. Among them were Miss Beatrice Harraden, Mr. Nevinson, Professor Surrey, and many others. One day those friends of hers surrounded me and asked me how was about the religions in Japan. That was a very difficult question to me. It is fact that I was at an American Missionary College in Japan and studied the Bible lessons for four years. But among us, the young school-

A JAPANESE ARTIST IN LONDON

boys, the Christians, were looked down as "not highly educated." I think the main reason was that those terribly ignorant and uneducated American missionaries in Japan were talking and doing too much nonsenses. While I was in America when anybody asked me if I were a Christian I always answered negatively to prove that I was not one of those "Uneducated." But to my astonishment I was entirely knocked down. They called me "Pagan," "Heathen," and "Barbarian," and they treated me as if I were not a human. Fancy! that one whose duty is supposed to be "to seek the lost sheep" should act himself not at all humanly!

Now, facing to my dearly respected English friends in Hampstead, I was rather too timid to express my own opinion so freely. Beside it was not my intention to injure the Christian faith in this country. So I shamefully acted myself as a fox. I said: "Japan is a free country for religions. You may find quite numbers of Christians there."

"How pity!" "How pity!" were the expressions from every one's mouth.

Some one shouted, "How about your beautiful philosophies, then?" Mrs. Dryhurst asked me, "Have you ever forgotten Laotze, Confucius, and Mencius?"

THE LOOSENING OF THE ROPE

I exclaimed, "Ahé, ahé. Wait, wait, wait, wait-a-second, please."

I could not speak immediately. When those ancient Chinese philosophers' names were mentioned, my heart was so deeply stricken with joy, as if one was told the name of a woman to whom he devoted his love. Indeed, Laotze, Confucius, and Mencius are my very best sweethearts in this world. I do not worship them as gods, but I heartily love them as my elderly brothers.

My first words to my friends was, "I am not a Christian." "You are right, you are right," was echoed and re-echoed in their mouth. Then I confessed how timid I was before them, and they all heartily laughed. Then I told them that my father was a great scholar of the Ancient Chinese Classics, and I was brought up with those philosophies together with Bushido. Therefore when I sunk into penniless poverty and suffered terribly, my philosophies were my own leaders.

Of course, those ancient philosophers did not always say original things. Many words of theirs I often found out already in my heart, but to see that they had same idea with me, was such a comfort. It is always so. For instance, I lost my mother when I was eleven years old. I was almost broken-hearted. Some

A JAPANESE ARTIST IN LONDON

doctors gave up hope of my life. At this moment I hated to see those sympathisers, who persuaded me to look " the bright side." Only one best companion of mine was a little boy, who lost his mother at the same time. We two used to seclude ourselves in a room and shed tears together. That was the sweetest moment then. Confucius or Mencius always wiped away my tears during my hard life.

Those friends of mine in Hampstead insisted that I should give the philosophical lectures there. I did so for several evenings.

Mrs. Dryhurst used to give her cook "holidays," in order to make Japanese dinner. I was the chief cook, and she herself and her daughters and some of her guests were my assistants. It was a great fun that some half-dozen peoples worked whole afternoon in her kitchen. I was much amused to go out shopping with a little basket. Her grocery was on the corner of the street. But one day I saw a new grocery shop only a few doors beyond. They had such nice fresh mushrooms, and much cheaper than the other's, too. I bought some there, and went back so proudly and told her " these mushrooms have no walkie-walkie to-day."

Mrs. Dryhurst was so angry with me, and said, " How dare you go to that new shop! I

THE LOOSENING OF THE ROPE

have been a customer of that old shop ever since I came to this house. They all know where you come from. You have done such a dreadful thing for me. Yes, I know that new shop sells better things for cheaper price. They are advertising themselves just now. You see, after a few weeks they will be just the same as the old shop, if not worse. I would rather eat 'walkie-walkie' than have things from the new shop."

Her lecture impressed my heart so much about the English Conservative.

I am not talking about the political sects now. Let them be Unionists or Liberalists, Nationalists or Socialists, all the Britons are so Conservative. This is most admirable. I remember it was only a few years ago hundreds of Chinamen came to London to establish a laundry. They worked nicer, cheaper, and quicker than English laundry. But all the Conservative Britons would not change their own laundry to the new comers. So the Chinamen were quite bankrupted and ran away. I think the Americans have much to learn from the Britons.

With such admiration in my heart, I became very faithful to Mrs. Dryhurst, and I used to go to her old shops every time. It was the time of the Russo-Japanese War. I went to buy

A JAPANESE ARTIST IN LONDON

some mushrooms at the old shop. The shopkeeper said the mushrooms were 8d. a pound. They were all eaten by insects and so bad, so I picked up only the good ones in a paper bag to weigh. The man made such a face with his round eyes, half amused and half perplexed, and said to me, " Nowadays Japan is having victories everywhere, sir. Even in my shop, sir ! "

I recognised that he could not be able to sell those I have left, because I had taken all the good ones. So I gave him twopence more, and he shook my hand with " Banzai."

As soon as I began to get a little work, to be able to pay for my daily bread, all sorts of illness visited me repeatedly. I had such bad " boils " on my neck, one after another. It was so painful. I could not lay down on bed. I used to pass several nights on the chair. I drowned myself with brandy to forget the pain, and a doctor was very cross with me and said, " that was the worst thing for the boils."

Blood-poison visited me next as the penalty of the bad food I had. Toothache, influenza, and intestine troubles were not modest enough to keep away from me. However, the ill-health and the bad weathers never affected on my tempers at all. The worst thing was, or is ever more, the insincereness of business peoples. Oh,

THE LOOSENING OF THE ROPE

those intentional insincerities on the matter of only a little payment! I often sunk into most disheartened condition, when I thought how faithless this world was. Arthur Ransome used to call on me most every day to cheer me up. And he and I went to the downstairs of Café de l'Europe on Friday evenings most regularly, he to find some idea to write, and I to sketch the peoples. I think he mentioned this in his book " Bohemia of London."

At this time I was not at all in " safe condition of my livelihood." Some kind-hearted person offered me a position as an artist for a lithographer firm. It was £3, 10s. a week. I absolutely refused this, because I knew it would stop my study altogether. Many of my friends were either angry with me or laughing at me. I got a name, " most foolish boy."

CHAPTER IX

"THE DARLING OF THE GODS"

It was the beginning of November 1903, when Mr. Spielmann told me that Sir Herbert Tree (Mr. Tree, then) was going to reproduce a Japanese play called "The Darling of the Gods." I might be a useful help for him. Did I care to work that? I answered him positively. Only a few days later I received a letter from Sir Beerbohm Tree, "Will you come to see us immediately?"

I went to the stage door of His Majesty's Theatre. First person I met there, was Mr. Michael Morton.

"What part of Japan do you come from?" was his question.

I answered most rapidly—"Aichi Ken, Mikawa no Kuni, Nishikamo-Gori Koromo cho O-Aza Koromo Aza Jimokudai."

I was sure that he could not catch a single word, but he showed a most satisfactory smile. Afterwards I learnt from him that he was rather afraid that I might not be a real

"THE DARLING OF THE GODS"

Japanese, because I "don't look like Japanese." Good gracious! I wanted so badly to show him my Keidsu (family tree), which my brother is keeping in Japan. With that family tree you can trace as far back as more than a thousand years, when my ancestor was a royal prince.

"Shika mo Seisei toto taru Seiwa-Gengi no Matsuyei nari Anakashiko, Anakashiko!" (At least, I am the descendant of the purest and most worshipful Gengi family, the true offspring of the Emperor Seiwa. Amen! Amen!)

Mr. Morton and I have become such great friends to each other now. Although I have made hundreds friends in London since then, whenever I count my very best friends in my one hand I always bend one finger for him. That is to say, he is one of the five best friends among hundreds. Wherever I go, he always tries to come and see me, and he was the frequentest visitor while I was in Paris.

Mr. Morton took me to Mr. Tree's dressing-room during the evening performance, and I saw Sir Beerbohm Tree first time as "Richard II."

Miss Lena Ashwell came into the room a few minutes later. She told me she was going to take a part in "The Darling of the Gods." A call-boy informed Mr. Tree, "Time, sir," again and again, and he was on and off the

A JAPANESE ARTIST IN LONDON

whole evening. We all had a little chat, hearing the cheering voices for "The Bolinbroke," "Thunders" at Wales Coast, the Bells of Westminster, and the Pipers outside the Tower of London, everything which was going on on the stage downstairs. Morton brought me to Mr. Dana's room, and we settled the "business matter." Gentler, easier and fairer than any business I had before! I said to myself, "Oh, I don't hate the business matter now! I see it does not always taste like castor oil. This is perfectly honey!"

From the next day I had to attend the rehearsal from eleven to four. I knew that Mr. Tree would not like any stranger to watch the rehearsal. But to my surprise I saw a strange gentleman sitting on one of the stall seats and watching us. He came to me and said, "How do you do, Mr. Markino?"

I looked at him quite curiously. He said, "I am Mr. Tree."

Oh, I was so much ashamed of myself. I have seen him ever so many times on the stage, but that was my very first time to see his private face, and I could not recognise him. Why, how could he transfigure himself such as Richard II. last night? He is most wonderful actor for "making up," and I renewed my amazement once more when he "made

"THE DARLING OF THE GODS"

up" himself as Zakuri. A real Japanese villain!

The way Mr. Tree and Mr. Morton drilled all those "extra" ladies and supers was wonderful. I can never forget their patientful task. They asked me to make them "real Japanese," and "to be very particular for everything, and not a bit of mercy for that." Every word of mine was the rule for them. I knew I was such a dreadful demon to them. Poor "extra ladies" so often had to sit on the hard floor half-an-hour, or even an hour, according how the rehearsal was going on. Those leading actors and actresses shared this torturing all the same. But they were so wonderful the way every one of them caught the real spirit of Japan.

There was a Japanese restaurant near Bloomsbury at this time. One afternoon I took Mr. Tree, Miss Ashwell, Miss Constance Collier, and Mr. Morton there. We sat down on cushions and ate Japanese dinner with chop-sticks. Mr. Tree said, "I really feel that I am Japanese," and I saw on the stage that he was as good as his words.

Miss Ashwell copied my sister so well from her photo. I often wished to call her my sister.

As the first night was approaching I began

A JAPANESE ARTIST IN LONDON

to be so busy. Besides the daily rehearsal, I had to look after costumes, coiffure, and scenery painting, to see if all the details were correct. Last few nights the rehearsal was going on as late as four or five o'clock in morning. I could not sleep more than four hours.

My actor friends used to invite me to "a Samurai dinner" at various restaurants. Yes, all were "Samurais"—mock Samurais of the prosperous English actors, and one real Samurai in miserable poverty.

I am still keeping the intimate friendship with some of these "Samurais."

Was the rehearsal of this play merely a pleasure to me? No, there was something more serious and more important for my life. I don't think I have ever told that even to Sir Beerbohm Tree before. Now let me confess it freely. It was such a valuable study for my art. It was a best chance to look all those pretty ladies and handsome actors so closely and to watch all their movements. Where else could I have such a chance? I stared at their faces and I stared at their figures all through the rehearsing time. Nobody thought of me vulgar, as it might happen so if I did the same at any public place, for it was my duty to rehearse them. And when I went back to my room I used

"THE DARLING OF THE GODS"

to draw them from memory. What a good life class it was!

Of course I was as faithful of my duty as possible. So my brain was twice busier than Mr. Tree was imagining.

After this play was put on I often visited the theatre to meet all my actress and actor friends. One evening while I was watching the play from the wing, the stage manager teased me to push me on the stage. I was so frightened that on the same night I had a nightmare, that I fell on the stage while the curtain was up. More than once I repeated this nightmare, and when I was awaken and found myself in bed I was so happy. I am sure that the stage manager's joke affected on my nerves too much.

CHAPTER X

I BECOME A CHELSEA CONSERVATIVE

At the same time that Japanese play was performed at His Majesty's Theatre, I had the special invitation from Walker's Art Gallery, as well as Bristol Academy, Manchester Gallery, &c., and I removed to No. 68 Sydney Street, Chelsea. The landlord's name was Mr. Bates. He had wife and two daughters and two sons. They were all such simple and kind-hearted peoples. They had a maid called Lottie. About this maid there was a pathetic story. She was a quite plain-looking, rather comical girl. I was almost astonished with her loyalty to her master and mistress. Wonderful, especially in Europe! (In Japan some servants have a great devotion to their masters, which European peoples cannot imagine.) One day, when I got more or less acquainted with those peoples, I asked about Lottie's life to one of the daughters, just for curiosity. And I was told that Lottie was a homeless child some thirty years ago, and

I BECOME A CHELSEA CONSERVATIVE

Mrs. Bates picked her up and brought her home. She was very clever. But when she was about nine years old, some wicked children knocked her head so hard that Lottie fainted. Since then she has been funny of her mind very often. She is so even now. But she is most faithful and sympathetic woman. She has been serving in this house for some thirty years, and she feels as if it is her own home. She has saved a few hundred pounds. But she has no pleasure for herself. If those young daughters talk something about love-matters, she always gives them her full sympathy, but always says, " Ah, it is not for me," and keeps herself back. She has absolutely given up her own life! What a wonderful decision she has! Nowadays there are so many nuns and monks. They are all in their own habits. But I wonder how many of them have no romantic feelings like this poor woman!

Is it because she recognises her own plain-looking? Or is it because her poor life? Does she not feel sad for herself? She seemed she did not. But I myself felt so sad for her. Whenever I saw her, the questions of humility puzzled my heart so deeply.

Ever since I removed to Sydney Street I began to feel very nervous about my future life. I am getting older and older every day, while my own art is still in such a beginning stage. Am I to pass all my life as an amateur artist? This question began to worry me so much that I could not sleep night after night. Something must be done at once—now or never!

I quite decided not to do pot-boilers any longer. Nothing but real study! Poverty was in sight very nigh to approach to me every day, but I paid no attention. I refused to do any of those uninteresting designs for a few pounds. I went into the study of London mists. How do I like London Mists? I have written that in my essay of "The Colour of London," so I am not going to repeat it here. Only one thing I must say. It is so difficult to get the real effect. I have never done it right yet. At the same time it is most interesting subject to study. I used to wander about the streets day and night. Sometimes twelve hours in a day. I was quite in a dream whenever I loitered outdoors.

One evening I started my place about nine o'clock and enjoyed myself in fogs until I felt my feet so tired that I came back to my conscience. I could not recognise where I was. I asked the passer-by what place was it. He said "Wimbledon." Why, I must

I BECOME A CHELSEA CONSERVATIVE

have passed over either Putney Bridge or Hammersmith Bridge then, and I had no memory of crossing bridge. It was after twelve, and I had to walk all way back.

Sometimes I started my place after midnight and walked about until sunrise. The more I observed the mists the more I fell into love. But it was most disappointing thing when I tried to put my impressions on paper. I could never be able to paint London fogs as I saw. I cursed my stupid hand. Every morning when I saw a white paper I had such a great anticipation to do something " grand," and after all day's hard work, I found out my paper only too hideous, and I threw it in the fire. Sometimes I repeated the same subject six or seven times, and when it was finished after five or six weeks it was simply unbearable to look at it. It was buried in the fire again.

At this time Mr. Lee Warner called upon me, and told me I must try to sell my works, even if they were not quite satisfactory. I said, " How can I do such things! Art is not same with butcher's business. Butchers could sell some inferior meats for low price to those poor peoples. Even if the meats taste rather nasty, it would stop the hunger of the poor and save their death from starvation. It is not so with Art. Such inferior Art like mine couldn't

A JAPANESE ARTIST IN LONDON

give any pleasure for Art-lovers. They would get sick of it. How could I claim even 1d. for my work? On the other hand, if I ever become to paint just as I wanted, I would not refuse even £1000, or £10,000. Will you wait until then?"

"Oh, don't be so silly, you must try to make money, or at least I must try for you."

He snatched away from me one sketch of "Egerton Mews in Mist" which I was going to put into the fire. And next day I got a registered letter from him, a six pound cheque in it.

I am afraid he betrayed me to my landlady, because she used to tell me, "Don't throw your pictures in fire, sir. Oh, please don't do that, sir." However, I made four or five pictures in one year time. Somebody gave me several introduction letters to show these pictures to them. I took one introduction letter with my portfolio to a lady. I rang the bell. A servant came out to the door. She took that letter to show to her mistress, and told me to wait, and she banged the door. I had to wait outside. It was such a hot summer day. The newly-painted door reflected the strong sun upon me. I felt I was in an oven. The perspirations made me wet all through. I was nearly cooked. I wanted

I BECOME A CHELSEA CONSERVATIVE

to go away immediately, but something whispered to my heart, " Be patient, for the sake of the one who so kindly wrote the introduction letter." It was only my little etiquette to him to wait. After about three-quarters of an hour the lady came to door and took my portfolio "in hope she might be able to buy some." All the pictures were returned to me next day.

Couldn't my life be any more than a pedlar? Will not this world give me bread unless I sell all my dignity? O, let me be starved to death! Such dirty breads shall never go down through my throat!

I burnt all the other introduction letters then, and I shed the bitterest tears in my room. Only my Ancient Chinese Classic book alone so soothingly comforted me at this moment. It told me what a hard life Confucius had. Once all the peoples hunted Confucius to kill him. He had a refuge with his faithful pupils in a wilderness for three days and three nights. He exclaimed, " Our ancient odes say, ' Not being a panther and not being a tiger, yet I have to pass my life in this wilderness.' Is my Tao (doctrine) wrong? Why should I be like this?"

Shiko, one of his pupils, said, " Our Master's Tao is extremely great. Nobody in this world could accept it." Gankai, another pupil, said, "Why should we worry because we are not accepted by this world? After not being accepted by this world, we can recognise that our Master's Tao is really great."

One day the maid came to my room and said, "Miss Griham wants to see you, sir."

Miss Graham? Why, her father and brother came to me through Mr. Lee Warner's recommendation, and they both bought my pictures lately, and I heard that Miss Graham was so kind to help me by every way she could. I told the maid to make my room look tidy (that was a great job for her, because I always keep my room in such disorder). While the maid was doing that I went into my bedroom and put on my old-new suit. The maid brushed me, saying, "Aint Miss Griham purty! Is she yer yung lydy, sir?"

"You must not be so rude. If the lady hear you she would take that as most insulting words. Remember she is a very, very aristocratic lady, and I think she came to help me."

"I-n-dee-d, sir."

She went down to ask Miss Graham to come up. I waited her on the top of the stairs. She was climbing up seventy-two stairs.

It took some time for her to reach the top floor. She looked about one foot shorter than

I BECOME A CHELSEA CONSERVATIVE

her real height. What a strange effect of perspective when one is seen from the top. Quite a new lesson to me! And what! The Hon. Miss Graham in a straw sailor hat? And in a plain cotton blouse? Whatever on earth has happened to her? Was she outcast by her father?

Lo! it was a quite strange person!

"Are you Miss Graham?"

"Yes, I am. I saw your address in *This Year's Artists*, so I have come."

"Ah, you are a model then?"

"Yes, sir."

It was awfully difficult for me to control my laughter. I told her I never use models, but if she was not very busy I should like to have tea with her. She came into my room and looked around with such a curious expression. My room was about three and a half by four yards.

"I suppose you have a studio somewhere else?"

"No, Miss Graham. This is my studio as well as my drawing-room. It turns into my dining-room thrice a day—oh, no, I am not quite sure of it—sometimes twice in a day and perhaps once in a day very often. But to-day let us call this my 'boudoir,' and we shall have tea together."

A JAPANESE ARTIST IN LONDON

I rang the bell for tea. Fancy all the trouble she had to find out my address and come to see me! Perhaps she might have had an air-castle to make a fortune through me—a half-starving artist! And, fancy! it was such a trouble I had to make my room tidy and put on my only one shabby "best" suit!

The maid brought the tea, and when she was leaving the room she made "eyes" on me with such a wicked smile. I could so plainly read her face then—"Is this yer very, very aristocratic friend?"

I told the pretty model that I myself was once a model. Over a cup of tea and a few cigarettes she told me all about her daily life. Some artists were very kind and some were very cruel, and that model is one of the hardest business in the world. "I believe," she continued, "Artist life is just as hard as model's." Poor, sympathetic, pretty girl! We could not materially help each other, but I was sure she had as much sympathy on me as my real aristocratic lady friend whose name was so singularly same. Wishing each other's luck, we parted after about two hours' pleasantest conversation.

My only one "best" suit could not endure all through my poorest life. The back of the

I BECOME A CHELSEA CONSERVATIVE

trouser was quite worn-out, and lo, such a big hole! It was all right in cold days, because I put on my overcoat when I went out. But on warm day I could not manage it well with the overcoat. I put some of my old socks inside the trousers and sewed them together. My maid said to me, "Your cloth look very bad, sir. You know Mrs. Bates is very kind to you; she would wait your payment, so you must make a new suit, sir."

Why, Mrs. Bates had already been kind enough to wait my debts some twelve or fifteen pounds, and I was quite penniless. It was absolutely impossible for me to buy a suit, and I was obliged to stop visiting to all my kind friends. I could not go to see even my worshipped Mr. Spielmann. He might have felt it rather strange that I used to write to him, while his flat was only five minutes' walk from my place. However, he has done all sorts of kindness by correspondence.

At this time my tailor's son came to see me. My tailor is Mr. J. J. Bax in Sloane Street. I knew him ever since I came to London. When I was living in Milner Street my landlady recommended him as a very best tailor, and I used to ask him to make all my clothes while I was working at the Japanese Naval office. Only a few weeks before I left

A JAPANESE ARTIST IN LONDON

the office I made one suit for credit, and as I began to sink into such poverty I could not pay that to him for these long five years, although I have always informed him my address whenever I changed, and he has not a single time pressed me hard.

Now his son visited on me. I was more than ashamed to see him. The son's name is Fred. When I saw him first time he was only a boy. I was surprised to see him so much grown-up.

"How could you forgive my most disgracefulness? I have been keeping my debts against you for a long five years. I feel so much ashamed to see your face."

"Oh, Mr. Markino, don't worry about that so much. But why don't you come to us to make more clothes? Surely you need more?"

He looked at my old suits. "Have you never made any suits since then? Is that all the suits you got?"

"Yes, this is all what I have."

"Oh, let us make one for you."

"No, my dear Fred, my debts to you have been already such a heavy burden on my heart. How could I double my debt to you? At present moment I cannot see when shall I be able to pay you, so let me be alone." And I told him how difficult it was to earn money from my pictures.

I BECOME A CHELSEA CONSERVATIVE

Fred Bax suggested that he would exchange suits with my pictures, but first of all he wanted to speak to his father. He took all my pictures with him.

In an hour's time he came back to me again. He turned me such a bright expression and said, " My father wants three pictures of yours. For these we shall cancel your £5 debt against us. Besides that, we shall make one lounge suit and one overcoat, and here I bring the cash of £2 to make the 'balance' for all. You must put this cash in your pocket and don't let your landlady know that, because you need some pocket-money."

Since this time Fred used to call on me very often to see how I was getting on, and every time he came, he used to leave a packet of cigarettes, for he knew so well that I was fond of smoking.

Nowadays, when I go to his shop to order some clothes, I always look at those three pictures hanged on his room and I recollect his kindness when I was so poor. About that cash of £2, I could not conceal them from my landlady. I gave all the money to her. She would not take them, saying, " You must keep them, as you don't know when you can get money next."

I said, " It is only too true that I don't know

when money comes to me next. Therefore you must have this."

After a long hesitation, my kind landlady took £1, 15s. for herself and left five shillings for my "pocket-money."

Very seldom I used to get a few pounds from my pictures, and whenever I gave that money to the daughter of my landlady she was so frightened to take them, and used to say, "Please wait, I must ask my Mamma about that." She would run down immediately. Then the mother came up and she always gave a few shillings change, notwithstanding I had some £20 debts against her.

One more or less fortunate day, I found out a letter on my breakfast table. I hurried to open it. Five penny stamps were in it. The letter started with "My dear Jack." Whoever is it to call me "My dear Jack"? It was very shaky handwriting. With such a great difficulty I read it through. The meaning of this letter was something like this. "The time is getting on very hard. You must suffer terribly. This is all what I could spare for you. I hope you will enjoy a good dinner with this."

It puzzled me awfully. The address above the letter was somewhere in New Cross. The sender's name was quite strange to me. I

I BECOME A CHELSEA CONSERVATIVE

picked up the envelope and found out it was not for me. It was addressed to *Mac . . . So-and-so*, 68 *S . . . So-and-so Street*. The postman misdelivered it and the maid thought it was for me. I was so sorry to open such a private, pathetic letter. Fancy, there are some peoples for whom fivepence is a "good dinner"!

Ah, I must not complain my own poverty. How many are suffering far more than myself! I had two penny stamps then. So I put these stamps in that envelope with the five stamps, and shut it up with a note "much apology for opening it by a mistake," and asked the maid to return it to the postman.

Mr. Douglas Sladen made arrangement at this time for me to submit my sketches to *The Queen* once or twice in a month. I remember it was when Mr. George Alexander produced "The Prodigal Son" at the Drury Lane, I got a wire from *The Queen*—" Go to Drury Lane and make full page sketch." The wire came to me at 1.5, and the curtain had to be raised at 2 o'clock. Alas! I had no penny for bus fare. I had to walk all the way from Sydney Street to the Drury Lane. It was such a hot summer day. When I reached there I was quite bathed in perspiration. The play was already going on. There was not a space on the standing room. At first I thought I would refuse this job! But I was so afraid *The Queen* might have to be published with a blank page, that I stretched my feet and peeped through the people's shoulders, and I made a sketch from my memory at home.

Although I had the payment of my sketches from *The Queen* I was still far away from any comfortable life. I used to owe my debts always over £10 against my landlady.

CHAPTER XI

SOME JAPANESE IMPRESSIONS OF ENGLAND

To my greatest delight, I got such good companions, two of my country-fellows, Hara and Wakamiya. Hara came to London to study art, and Wakamiya to read the books at British Museum. I would not be surprised if Wakamiya has read all the books in the Museum during his stay in London. At least, it is quite sure he has read the books there, which he felt necessary.

These two Japanese friends used to call on me from time to time. I was in such a strange position that they used to make me a second person and not the first person like themselves, when we talked about the English customs. Indeed they looked upon me as if I were an English person, and questioned me many things about English life. Sometimes we all agreed each other so well, and sometimes we had such dead-heat discussions until midnight, or even until the next morning.

The English readers of this book might feel

A JAPANESE ARTIST IN LONDON

curious to know what we Japanese were talking together, on the little top-floor room of 68 Sydney Street. Therefore I have made one chapter here especially about the topics of our conversation.

Though the cranes have such long legs they would lament if we cut one-tenth of an inch off them. Though the ducks have such short legs they would grieve if we add half an inch on them. Different nations have entirely different ideas, and whether their own ideas are too long or too short, they are always at their utmost comfort with their own way. We, the strangers, have no right to argue any English customs with the English peoples.

What I am going to write here is my own idea. The readers might be offended with me. But I sincerely wish to the readers, that as I am always looking upon England as my second home, you will not hurt your friendly feeling toward me, whatever I say which must be strange to your ears.

Sometimes Hara and Wakamiya brought one or two more Japanese. Now I don't remember which of them said which. I remember they often told me their own impressions, which I thought most splendid. But I feel I have no privilege to write what they said without their consent. Let us hope they themselves will write their own ideas some day.

"What do you think of the English free marriage?"

"I think that is no better, whatever they say. People say they marry by their own love. That sounds awfully comfortable, but I often wonder how many of them really know what is love. So many times I have seen terrible results through the free marriage. The people are as unhappy as could be. Even during their honeymoon they often quarrel each other. Where is their love after all? In the average, un-harmonial and unhappy families are no less in England than in Japan. Perhaps some of them might be in a deep love when they married. But remember England has a proverb—'Love is blind.' Indeed, some of them are too blind, and when they begin to open their eyes that is only the beginning of the quarrel. I am afraid such quarrels are the bitterest ones. On the other hand, parents are not always so blind, therefore the fixed marriage of the parents often makes their young children happier than the children themselves are imagining. I say this especially for those who marry very young. The fixed marriage by the parents could not always be happy, but there is some duty in their hearts. I myself know several Japanese who married by their parents' will. First they could not love each other, but they never forgot to be loyal to their parents. For the sake of their parents they never quarrelled, but always forgave each other, and in their later life they became most harmonial. We cannot see such beautiful ethics in England.

"Then, again, I often feel so sorry for young Englishwomen for their custom of free marriage. So many young men go after them, especially if the women are beautiful, and they annoy them too much. How wonderful are those John Bullesses who manage all their difficulties so well. If I were they my face would have hundred wrinkles in a few years, but is it not simply miracle that they keep their faces so fresh like newly blossomed flowers, as if they have never met any annoyance?"

"Ah," my friend interrupted, "only if no young men come to them, they will get enough wrinkles in their faces."

"Pray don't disturb me with your witty jokes, for I am talking very seriously. I know some English young ladies who were much annoyed by some young men. I really sympathised with them. I know too well how awful it must be. Once I myself had an experience. Some lady whom I could not love chased after me, and I was so much annoyed."

Here all my friends laughed at me.

One of my friends said he could see so plainly one thing in London as the result of the free marriage. "It seems to me," he said, "that all nice-looking women marry quite soon. And somewhat plain-looking women are left alone. These women need some independent means for their life. That is why we don't see many beauties among lady artists or writers."

I said, "That is rather cruel judgment. Because I know several lady artists who are most charming and beautiful. Besides, if some artists or writers look rather plain, there is a great cause. I am a man, but how much am I suffering to reach to the goal as an artist! Women must suffer more than men, because the former are more sensitive than the latter. Most charming girl shall be turned into plain-looking woman by the time she succeeds as an artist or a writer, and surely such women often miss the chance of marriage only because they are too earnest to their own ambition."

About the social life of English men and women, I used to praise that to my Japanese friends. The scholars of Confucius said, "Men and women must be separated in different rooms since six years of their age." They said this evidently because they were afraid of any impropriety. I must decidedly say they were mistaken. If you keep any difficulty aside the longer, the more will be the difficulty. It is not only about the different sexes but it is so with everything. One who faces towards any difficulty the sooner always conquers it the sooner. The English life shows it to me. I have noticed more than once that when I have had walk with a woman of the different nationality she gave me a queer feminine feeling. But with my English lady friends I always feel as if they were my own sisters or schoolmates. John Bulless is the best to keep on the pure friendship.

Now, talking of this subject, I must say a few words about the pictures of nude figures. Why do some peoples say the nude figures are improper ? Look at those savage nations who have no clothes ! Have they more vulgar passions than we have ? I don't think so. If possible I wish all the ladies would be quite nude. There is nothing more graceful than the human figure. Those best dressmakers may be able not to destroy the beauty of the natural figure but they cannot help it by any means. Any smart dressmaker in Bond Street or in Rue de la Paix could not cut dress as graceful as the nude. They cannot make dresses better than the natural figure.

If the readers doubt me, ask any serious art

JAPANESE IMPRESSIONS OF ENGLAND

student in life class. They shall surely approve my logic. Only one thing I sincerely object to, is those poorly cut dresses which are so often too vulgar to look at.

I am very keen to read the divorce cases in the daily papers. Readers, are you shocked at me? Perhaps you are, but it is quite true. Now let me write why. I myself don't understand why clergymen or any ethical peoples don't read them. There is much to learn from the divorce cases. They are not the dreams or fantasies of novelists, but the real facts which are actually going on around us every day. They are not laughing or sneering matter, but most serious human philosophy. Fancy! Your own sisters and brothers are actually having such life around you! I must call those peoples " paradise-fools " who read only nice articles and hate to read the divorce cases. Why do peoples laugh when I talk about love? And then why don't they get rid of it either? When the humans are in graceful love there seems to me nothing could be nobler, and when they mislead their love, they are uglier than pigs or donkeys. Whenever I read the divorce case, I am always studying how their love was stolen away. My Japanese friends and I often had the question, which would be greater crime, the one who commits misconduct by temporary temptation, even if he or she is quite faithful in other respects, and the one who controls his passion yet devotes his or her heart absolutely to the co-respondent?

We often spent whole evening for this discussion. My own idea is that the former is savage animal, who has really "unsounded mind," quite different from the peoples who commit suicide, and the latter is intentional insincerity. The intentional insincerity must be a crime, yet too often a very pitiable condition exists in it too, and sometimes its condition is only too foolish. I was often told that I must not mix my philosophy with the laws. Ah, then, what is the law? Are we made to adopt ourselves to the law, or is the law made to adopt it to our life? This question is exactly the same as saying, "Is the language made for the grammar or the grammar made for the language?"

If the law is made for our life, the law must be same with our cloth. Could we wear the same cloth all the time? Indeed we are growing every day; how could we wear the cloth which we made when we were children? Certainly we cannot adopt the law of a hundred years ago to our modern life. The last question is, how long could we be under one same law?

One of my friends used to sigh and say,

JAPANESE IMPRESSIONS OF ENGLAND

"I don't understand the life of those city clerks. They go to the office every morning. They come back every evening. What is their pleasure beside eating and sleeping? Do they really know what human life is?"

I said, "They must have 'a life' with their wives."

"But," he said, "I often see some of them are quarrelling with their wives."

I said, "Perhaps they enjoy their children."

My friend asked, "Ah, could they not be any more than the human manufacturing machines, then?"

I said, "The human manufacturing machines are very important for the country. Any country never feels it has too many soldiers or sailors."

At this moment, one voice broken in from a corner. "How cruel you are, my dear friend! Do you mean to make them as cattle? you know it is the butcher's business to breed the cattles and kill them. Now do you really expect the Government should act to the nation as the butchers to the cattle?"

"But my own idea is always that if peoples could sleep without locking their doors, they would love that comfortableness. But as long as there are robbers and thieves in this world, we are all obliged to lock our doors. Is there any one lamenting, because we are wasting most useful metal like iron for making the locks? If one who has taste makes a little artistic touch on the locks they would be not merely the protection for thieves, but very nice decoration too. So with the sailors and soldiers! They can be the nicest decorations of their countries, and I am sure they are feeling that they have 'Life.'"

All my Japanese friends, as well as I myself, always very much praised the night school system in London. How splendid that one can study the scientific theories in the evening classes, while they practise all what they are learning on the daytime, and at the same time, make money for their own livelihood. Academical students often succumb themselves into too much science, so they are less practical, while the bread-makers often become ignorant of all the theories. The night schools combine these together to make one quite perfect.

One evening, my Japanese friend said to me, "It seems to me as the general rule that in every country in this world, the lower middle-class peoples are keeping the highest morals. The highest and richest class peoples are just as bad as the lowest and poorest class peoples. I suppose England is no exception to this rule?"

"Certainly England is no exception. But my own opinion is a little different. It is true that the middle-class peoples are behaving themselves best. But it is a great question, whether could I call them the highest moral or not. Once I kept a cat. She used to steal foods. Every time when she acted thief I used to smack her hard. In a few weeks' time, she began to behave herself so well, because she was afraid to be smacked again. Could I call that cat very loyal to me?

"The only one thing quite sure was that she did not annoy me. So with the middle-class peoples. They give no annoyance to this world. Perhaps their systematical life gives the pleasure to the Government, very much indeed. But, to talk frankly, I think many of them are very artificial, while the highest and the lowest class peoples are natural. The highest peoples are very natural, because they have money enough, and they can do just as they like. The lowest peoples are quite natural as well because they are in despair, and have no hope to elevate their own life. Only the middle-class peoples alone have the ambition to climb up. These sorts of peoples are always thinking not to be cast away from the social life. Perhaps they may meet with great temptation, but they control themselves so well,

A JAPANESE ARTIST IN LONDON

not for their religious heart, but for the fear that they might lose the next day's bread. Look at the life of clerks. They cannot get their good position unless they have some good references, and to get good references they must 'behave' themselves well. I suppose one who served 'hard' once, shall never be able to return his post again. I know so many of this class people. They are so timid and so trembling in their daily life as if they are walking on thin ice in order not to be drowned! At this moment how could they be natural? Accordingly their moral is more like some rough wood covered with varnish than some well-planed and polished wood. Varnished wood often looks smoother than any self-polished wood. But the latter is much safer. Indeed, I have seen so often that the varnish was cracked and some ugly grain appeared from the inside. How many times have I wondered that those supposed to be 'very sweetest friends' should have acted such mean thing about a little money matter upon me!

"On the other hand, I have seen so many sympathetic peoples who were trying to perish their own beautiful nature by all means and to keep themselves as cool as possible. Confucius said, 'Those who are desiring nothing but to be rich, shall never understand my

JAPANESE IMPRESSIONS OF ENGLAND

doctrine.' I remember Christ said something quite same in Bible, too. It is very difficult to find a real friend among these peoples. That is why I have more friends among the highest and the lowest classes, who are so natural. Look at the playgoers. Any pathetic tragedies are always unpopular among the middle-class peoples. They always mock at them and say, 'Oh, this is too heavy,' 'Oh, that is too silly.' They are trying not to be drawn into any pathetic feeling, which would be the greatest danger against their own ambition."

My Japanese friends remarked to me that it is most unavoidable result in such a thickly populated town like London. They must struggle like that, or else they shall become prey of the others.

May I introduce my cats here once more?

When I was in San Francisco, my landlady had a mother cat and one baby cat. These two cats were such great friends to each other. But we all had to go away for a few weeks' summer holiday. The landlady asked our neighbour to look after our cats. When we came back after the holidays, I was so surprised to see that the mother cat and baby cat were so severely fighting. They became such great enemies to each other. I have discovered that our neighbour did not give enough food

A JAPANESE ARTIST IN LONDON

to them. I sincerely ask the readers, shall we have to fight with our best friends when our foods are getting scarce? Are we the same class animals as cat? I cannot help without recollecting the kindness of those landladies of most common lodging-houses where I passed my poor life. Without their noblest conduct, I could not enjoy my life to-day.

It was one of these days I was reading an evening paper, and all my Japanese friends came. There was a news of a murder case. I think it had occurred in a lonely country somewhere about Tottenham (I forget where it was). Anyhow, one young farmer had shot his neighbour. There was no witness except his own father. The father so dearly loved his only one son. Of course it was the gravest news to him. But when the father stood in the witness-box and kissed the Bible, he gave all evidence against his own dear child, and afterwards he was broken down. I put the newspaper on my desk and said, "Why should the father give witness against his own son? If I were he, I would refuse to go to the witness-box!"

One of my Japanese friends sighed deeply, and said, "Perhaps in such a case I too may have the same idea with you. But just bring your thought one step further. That English father certainly had the nobler moral.

JAPANESE IMPRESSIONS OF ENGLAND

I must admire the English custom most seriously."

We often talked about the religions too.

My idea is that peoples ought to stick to the religion in which they were born and brought up, because it ought to come to them most natural. It is the sweetest part of the human life. Indeed, the religions could not be served by any logic. If one tries to attack other's faith by his own logic, he would only injure the sweetest and tenderest part of the heart of his friend. But here I have a few things to mention. Those early Christians were most wonderful. What could be more beautiful than those faiths for which they sacrificed their own lives? Here is the translation of a Japanese poetry. " Mostly everything in this world seems to be false, yet one who gives up his life for anything must be really sincere."

But nowadays most of those so-called earnest Christians are nothing more than the masked hypocrites. I have had much experience with these sorts of peoples. There is another kind of Christian who is not so bad as those hypocrites. But their faith is so miserably shallow. They say, " Oh, that is God's will," or " Oh, this is God's will." They bring everything to God too quickly. When they go to

A JAPANESE ARTIST IN LONDON

this extremity they begin to feel that doctors are not needed for their illness. If they see one whose heart is aching with misery, they so cruelly mock at it and say, "O, you have no faith to God." These sorts of Christians often become so proud before the outside people, and they often mock us and call us with bad names. What great traitors to Christ!

I sincerely ask them, "Hasn't God given us our head and heart to think and to feel?" If flowers were blossomed directly on a big trunk of tree they would not be quite so beautiful. Don't you think some long slender stalk makes the blossoms so beautiful? Let us hope that the stalk between God and us is as long as possible. That is the way to make our mutual life so sweet. Perhaps to shed tears whole evening for the sake of our friends is one of the sweetest moments of our life.

Do you say our food is only for appetite, and would you swallow it? Only very low-class animals do so. We human beings must grind the food with our teeth and taste it very carefully, whether it may be sour or sweet.

Some great Buddhist priest in Japan said, "Those who talk too much of Buddha with their mouths are not real Buddhists. The real Buddhism dwells in the hearts of those who are silent."

JAPANESE IMPRESSIONS OF ENGLAND

I think I can apply these words to the Christianity too.

I have several English friends who are always silent, but I can see most beautiful Christianity in their hearts.

Now let me write a few more of our conversations.

"I say, Markino, don't you think the London cabmen are awfully stupid? Whenever I get in cab, the cabman never understands where I want to go. He always asks me my destination again and again."

"My dear friend, if cabmen were clever enough to understand your broken English so quick as you want, they would not be cabmen. But I teach you one thing. You tell your cabman from next time the name of a 'pub' near by your destination, he will understand you at once."

"Well, but don't you think those cabmen or bus-drivers talk so vulgar when they were struck by something passing by? They sound simply awful."

"Ah, that is their own natural sound. Do you beat a slack drum and expect to hear the sound of a nice bell? Have you not seen those salesmen ring your coin on the desk whether it sounds the real gold or forgery? If you want to know anything or anybody's real

A JAPANESE ARTIST IN LONDON

nature, just strike them; they will always give the sound of their own nature."

"I say, Markino, what do you dislike most in London?"

"The servants' breath. I don't know why, but when those servants talk to me, they generally put their faces so near to mine and shout so loud. I have to inhale all disgusting odour of their breath."

"Hear, hear; we are experiencing that uncomfortable job, too. The best way to avoid it is to tell them we are not deafs, so we can clearly hear their low whispers from far away."

"Oh, then, Markino, what do you like most in London?"

"The safety in the midnight. Wherever in this world is such a safe town like London? You can walk anywhere in London at any time in night. You need not have any fear at all. This is awfully convenient to me to study the night effect."

"I say, Markino, don't you feel it is more like a shop than a drawing-room when you go to the English house? They put all their properties on their drawing-rooms."

"I love both way, Japanese as well as English. It is only different taste, that is all. Certainly it is very artistic taste to have only one genuine Kakemono on the Tokonoma,

JAPANESE IMPRESSIONS OF ENGLAND

and it concentrates all our eyes there. It gives me a very pleasant feeling. But on the other hand, I don't object the English idea at all. When they are arranged beautifully it is awfully nice. Besides, we must think how long could we live in this world. Suppose one had more than five hundred pictures, and he was keeping them in Japanese way, how many times could he see the same picture in his life? How pity to hide some pictures or curios which he so dearly loves. When I think this point, I like the English way quite well."

CHAPTER XII

MY JAPANESE FRIENDS

After Wakamiya went back, some young Japanese students, Oku and Hidaka, arrived from Japan, and Hara and Oku removed to my lodging to live together, and Hidaka was the frequent visitor. Until my Japanese friends removed to my place, they did not know all about my poverty, for my landlady was such a kind woman, and she always served teas, dinners or suppers to all of us whenever they came, notwithstanding I was in a heavy debt against her. She did not want me "to look too shabby." But now they were with me day and night.

Perhaps nobody could understand Japanese better than Japanese. They at once found out that I went to bed without supper every night. Their nature was only too tender and too delicate. They did not want to help me in any way which I might have taken as "insulting." Hara came to me and said,

MY JAPANESE FRIENDS

"Do you know, Markino, I cannot have my supper in my room?"

I said, "Oh?"

"No, I could not," he continued. "That gas-stove gives bad odour, and I lose all my appetite. May I have my supper in your room? But do I disturb you? Tell me if I do."

Two suppers were already ordered. The maid used to bring them to my room. "Kindly keep company with me," was the most courteous word of Hara. Although I was so much moved with his kindness I intentionally did not express my thanks to him, for I knew it was not his desire. On the contrary, I often told him it was "a great disturbance to me" to have supper together, and asked him to have his supper in his own room.

Oku and Hidaka often said to me, "We want so much to go to some west-end restaurants, but we cannot read the menu, and we are too shy to go there ourselves alone. Will you kindly take us to those restaurant?" Sometimes I accepted it for the sake of "their pleasure," and sometimes I refused, saying they ought to be ashamed of themselves for to be so "shy."

Now I sincerely apologise to my Japanese friends for mentioning that in this book, for

A JAPANESE ARTIST IN LONDON

I know too well that they would not like that. Only if I were in Japan I should not utter a single word about that. But in England I always feel I am an interpreter between English and Japanese, and I want to introduce to all the English readers the different morals of Japanese peoples.

This is only a brief sketch of their kindness. They have done most innumerous kindness to me, which I shall not disclose here. The day might come that I might forget that delicate taste of these dinners, but their sweetest, tenderest, and most delicate kindness to me shall I never forget.

Once in a week we used to have Japanese dinner. It was our greatest fun. After whole day's work we all went out for shopping the materials—such as beef, chickens, fishes, turnips, carrots, mushrooms and rices. We were loaded with bundles. Very often the bags were broken on the street, and all those turnips were rolling over the pavement. We picked them up with such laughter, but if too many English peoples were watching us, we were so shy, and we left them on the street, and ran up to home as quick as possible.

Oku's room was our kitchen. After we brought back all the materials, we asked the maid to lend us several saucepans, a pastry-

MY JAPANESE FRIENDS

board, and knives. We spread out some newspaper on the table and prepared the food, and cooked everything on the fireplace. We did not want anybody to come into our "cooking" room. The door had no key, so we used to put several chairs against the door. But the maid had such enormous strength; she often pushed the door open. Then all the chairs tumbled over, and such a confusion it was. Just like an earthquake! We were so shy, and we hid ourselves behind the covers and screens.

To us, our ill-cooked Japanese dishes were far more delicious than those dinners at Savoy or Carlton. I often ate too much, and I could not move. "Oh, pray don't make me laugh! It's simply torture to me. I feel such a pain!" I was really a pig.

The most valuable friendship I had with Hara, was not only with his delicate sympathy on my poverty, or any discussion about the English life. There was something more. That was because he was such an accomplished and sincere artist. The very first day he came to see me I noticed he was playing his pencil on a piece of paper all the time while we were talking, then he crunched it and threw it into my waste-paper basket and went off. For curiosity, I picked up that paper after he went

A JAPANESE ARTIST IN LONDON

away and looked at it. Why, there was such wonderful portraits of mine! Some profiles and some full faces with decided likeness, and some whole figures with all my personal mannerism caught so accurately. The full admiration and respect towards him was grown in my heart at once. "Ah, surely his art is much elder than mine. How very lucky to get such a friend!"

But he himself was so modest and so earnest and so sincere to the art. First few weeks I used to take him round the streets, and whenever we passed some picture shops he stopped to look through the shop window, and he would not move on. I told him those nameless artists' works were not half as good as his own. But he always said, "Oh, please don't say so. Perhaps my drawings are surer than those, and my compositions are better too. But the European artists know how to use oils so skilfully. I learn great lessons from them."

Although I myself am such a great admirer of Turner now, I was not so until Hara came. In fact, I hated Turner. Just a few days after Hara arrived in London, he and I went to the National Gallery and sat down on the seats in the Turner's room.

I said to him, "The greatest heroes in this world were generally the greatest deceivers.

MY JAPANESE FRIENDS

Don't you think Turner was one of the greatest heroes and deceivers?"

"Why?"

"Why, come and look at this picture of Trafalgar Battle. Look at these figures! Look at Nelson! What an awful drawing! I think even ten year old child could draw better figures. Oh, Turner was such a speculator!"

Hara was in silence.

"Do open your mouth and tell me your opinion."

"My opinion? I have no opinion at the present moment. Everything is so different from what I anticipated in Japan. I feel I am dreaming, and I feel as if fox is in my head. So pray leave me quite alone. Only one word I want to tell you. That is, I appreciate your sincereness. Turner is known as one of the greatest artists in the world. Everybody says 'Turner, Turner, and Turner.' But how many of them really understand why Turner is a great artist. Now you don't like Turner, and you express that so freely. I like you so much because you are not a bit conceited."

Hara began to copy Rembrandt in the National Gallery. He went there twice a week quite regularly. One whole year passed by. One evening he came back from the National Gallery and said to me, "Now I have really found

A JAPANESE ARTIST IN LONDON

out that Turner is very, very great. I say this with all my own confidence and responsibility."

Since this evening he used to tell me how much love he is in with Turner. I hated him to talk of Turner like that, and whenever he began to talk of Turner I used to turn the topic of our conversation into Russo-Japanese War with Oku.

Hara sighed deeply. "My poor friend, if you can not love Turner, you can not be a great artist. For you, Turner is more important than the war news."

"Oh, shut up, Hara, I hate Turner; you are not allowed to say Turner in front of me."

It was just the time that all those small works of Turner's were put in Tate Gallery. Hara came back from the Tate and asked me —" My dear friend, will you honourably accept my humble invitation to a worthless luncheon to-morrow?"

I answered him, "My dear friend, I most humbly accept your honourable invitation."

"Ah, then, you must go to the Tate at the same time and look at those Turners with me for my pleasure."

I was well cornered, I could not refuse it. I asked him whether he wanted me to go to the Turner's room before or after the luncheon. He said he did not mind either way.

MY JAPANESE FRIENDS

I said, "If I see Turner before the luncheon I shall lose all my appetite, and if I go there after the luncheon it would be seriously dangerous. Oh no, not after the meal, please!"

However, we went to the Tate after the luncheon next day. Hara led me into the Turner's room. I cannot express my feelings I had at that moment. Neither my Japanese nor my English (very sadly both are quite broken!) shall be able to express it. I think I was so strongly impressed by those wonderful Turners especially because I began to struggle to paint my favourite London fogs at that time. I watched one picture more than twenty minutes, then I had "go around," then I went back to some certain pictures again. Those wonderful atmospheric effects! The colours were breathing! The tones were moving! I had quite forgotten myself until the closing time came. I noticed somebody was standing behind me. Thinking it was Hara, I began to talk Japanese. But no answer! I looked back. He was a strange English man. Where was Hara? The porter said, "Your Japanese friend slipped off a long time ago!"

When I came back to my place, Hara shook my hand most warmly.

"So, you love Turner more than myself now.

A JAPANESE ARTIST IN LONDON

You were talking with Turner, and you have quite forgotten me. I am so glad, because you were quite right. Now I suppose you would not mind if I ask you to go to the National Gallery and see those Turners?"

"Would not mind? Why, I should like to go there with you so badly."

We both went to the National Gallery next day. All the Turners looked to me quite different. Hara said to me, "Look at those figures and horses. As you told me one year ago, they are very much like an amateur's work. But if you doubt whether was Turner good draughtsman or not, go downstairs, or go to South Kensington Museum and look at his water-colour study. What could he not have done? Indeed, those studies show that Turner was very accurate about his drawings. But I am sure he became very conscious that too accurate drawings give rather vulgar feeling, just like those cheap illustrations in some periodicals. Therefore he wanted to avoid all those possibilities of vulgar minute details. How noble and how high his art was!"

I thoroughly agreed with Hara. Thanks heartily to my dear friend Hara. He made my blind eyes open so that I could see the wonderful arts of Turner!

MY JAPANESE FRIENDS

With his sincerity and eagerness Hara was progressing his art day by day, and after three years he became to understand the European art most thoroughly. I remember Mr. Spielmann reproduced his copy of Rembrandt, together with the original, in *Graphic*, and he wrote most flattering articles. Even now Mr. Spielmann often tells me that "your friend Hara has seen most inner side of those masterpieces in the National Gallery."

Lately he wrote me from Japan. This is the translation:—

"Ever since I came back to Japan I have been so busy to see all those old Japanese masterpieces again to compare them with European art. I think now I understand them. How often I wished you were with me to look at those wonderful works! Nowadays all the Westerners have begun to take notice with our old arts. But I am afraid they are generally so miserably mistaken. I feel it is our duty to write a book on this subject. Let us do that some day soon."

CHAPTER XIII

"THE COLOUR OF LONDON"

It was on 20th of June 1906, a few of my best English friends made an arrangement for me to make a book from my pictures, and Mr. Loftie was to write the text. The name of the book was "The Colour of London," and Messrs. Chatto & Windus were to publish it. I hesitated to undertake this, because I felt my art was not quite perfect yet. But my friends told me that I must not always be so "foolish," so I started my work at once. All my Japanese friends were more delighted than I myself.

Although the publishers were kind enough to forward me some money by weekly payment, I had still some debts to my landlady, and I could not afford my bus fare every day. So I used to walk all the way wherever I went to sketch. My doctor friend told me afterwards that I had not lost anything by walking. It was very good thing for me. Because I needed daily exercise.

Anyhow, I was very glad to think that I

"THE COLOUR OF LONDON"

have to devote my life entirely on the real art. No more pot-boilers! As I began to feel some comfort on my daily life, I started to go round to see all my friends. My old friend Arthur Ransome and I often visited our artist friends, Alphaeus Cole and Miss Coleman Smith in Fulham. Then I visited on Mr. Spielmann more frequently, where I was introduced to many leading artists, writers and diplomatists. I was quite an earnest auditor to their very interesting conversations. Perhaps I was most spoilt at Mr. Sladen's house. Only he and Miss Lorimer were so cross whenever I spilt my cigarette ashes on the floor.

Oh, at his house I have met many jolly John Bulls and John Bullesses. I can not write all in this chapter. I am thinking some day to write a book exclusively about my John Bulless friends. Some one whispered me that I ought not. Why not? Why could I not write all my admiration about them? It is only pure and sincere admiration of them!

"The Colour of London" was published on May 8, 1907, and at the same time I had an exhibition of my original pictures at Clifford Gallery in Haymarket. On the opening day so many prominent peoples came. I was so shy, and I kept myself very small at one corner whole morning. But they began to

A JAPANESE ARTIST IN LONDON

flatter me and pet me. Only too kind of them to do so with such horrid works. Anyhow, I got some courage at last to face with all the visitors. I was surprised of myself on getting so bold.

Many flattering letters were pouring upon me, and I was invited to teas, dinners, theatres, and clubs. His Majesty the King so graciously accepted a copy of "The Colour of London."

My gay life did not last more than five days. It was a Saturday night, May 11th. I went to see one of my Japanese friends who was going home. Some half-dozen of my countryfellows had Japanese dinner together. Soon after the dinner, at midnight, I became seriously ill so suddenly. I had a cab-drive to my own lodging.

All night I was groaning in bed. As soon as the maid got up I asked her to wire to all my Japanese friends, Hidaka, Hara, and Oku, who have left my lodging a little time ago. Also I wired to Dr. Baldwin in Manchester Square.

I was acquainted with Dr. Baldwin before, because he and his brother were the admirers of my works, and bought some pictures.

My Japanese friends arrived to my room immediately. The doctor's servant replied that he was away to country, but he will attend on me as soon as he comes back.

"THE COLOUR OF LONDON"

All day long my Japanese friends nursed me with great anxiety. Their moisted eyes were better medicine than anything, and I forgot all my pain.

They suggested me that I ought to mention the name of my illness to the doctor, so that he would bring all necessary instrument. "Do you know, Markino, what is your illness called in English?"

I said, "This must be appendicitis."

"Are you quite sure?"

"Yes."

My friends wired the doctor, "Prepare all your instrument for appendicitis."

Dr. Baldwin came to my place with such a large bag with him in the evening.

He said, "Now let me see. Will you lay yourself upward."

"No, no, doctor; my illness is on my back."

"What? I say, Mr. Markino, this is not appendicitis. You have grossly deceived me. Look at what a job I have had to carry all those instruments in my bag!"

"But, doctor, I really thought 'appendicitis' was the right name in English."

He laughed so heartily, and said the real English name of my illness is ———. He had a temporary treatment for me, and said, "That will do for a few days, but you need an opera-

A JAPANESE ARTIST IN LONDON

tion. You had better go to the West London Hospital, where I myself shall operate you. You will get a card from the hospital in a few days. Until then you must wait."

I suppose my illness was the result of the bad foods and the lack of exercise through my poverty.

CHAPTER XIV

IN THE WEST LONDON HOSPITAL—BEFORE
THE OPERATION

A FEW days afterwards I received a card from the West London Hospital. The card said I must be at the door of the hospital at 10 A.M. on May 21st, just the next day of Whitsun Bank Holiday.

I drove a cab there quite punctually and presented the card to the porter. He asked me my full name and age and occupation, and my religion.

"My religion? I have none!"

He said, "Um . . . m, you are a Freethinker then?"

"Yes, will that do?"

"Yes, that will do quite well. You must go into the 'Accident Ward' and see the sister."

I entered into the ward with my little dressing bag. The sister gave me a bed, Number 12.

By a glance at this ward-room my very first impression was something which I can not express by any word. My heart was shuddered.

A JAPANESE ARTIST IN LONDON

" A quite different world altogether," was my first exclamation in my heart. Every patient in bed looked so deadly pale. Perhaps the light green walls made them look more so.

The ward-room was on the ground floor. It was a long room, its four windows on one side facing on the street, and the four windows on the other side facing to a corridor. Twelve beds were placed all around the room. No. 1 was starting from the nearest one to the entrance door, and No. 12 was by the entrance door again. In the middle part of the room a stove was placed. Beyond the stove was a large table for the sister to write the reports. Half of this table was covered with many flowers, which were given to the patients by some kind sympathisers. A few evergreen palms were spread high above these flowers. They seemed to tell me that " all those beautiful flowers in this world shall fade away quite soon. It is very sad thing, but it is so true. Only the pure, simple, and sincere green leaves live for ever and ever."

This ward-room had two wings at the bottom. One was for bath-room and the other for washing dishes, and making tea and beef-tea. Everything was so neat and clean, I was quite astonished at it. How could it be possible in this smoky London !

TOMBSTONE DESIGNED BY MARKINO

FLOWER SALES GIRL

HOME OF THE CHELSEA CONSERVATIVE: 68 SYDNEY STREET

MARKINO'S FRIEND, HARA

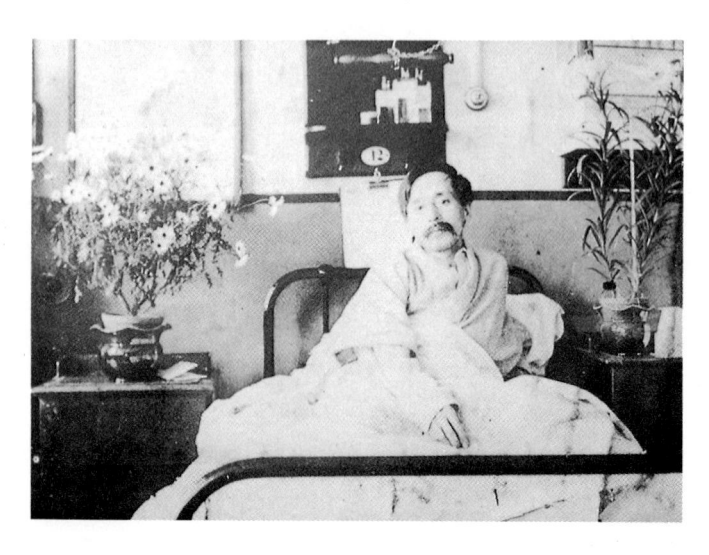

MARKINO IN THE WEST LONDON HOSPITAL

IN THE WEST LONDON HOSPITAL

I had a fish luncheon on the first day. After the luncheon Dr. Baldwin came and told me that I was going to be operated on Thursday afternoon.

From three to four I was allowed to go out to the back garden. There was a man on No. 11. He was nearly convalescent, though he looked so pale and weary. He and I went out together. He could not walk down a few step stairs, so I carried him on my back.

"Do I walk too quick?"

"Oh no, that's all right."

"Give me your right arm round my neck. That's it."

"Oh, my legs are so stiff; do I weigh you down too much?"

"Not at all."

We sat down together on a garden bench. The garden was about ten yards square and quite secluded from the outer world by a high wall, and the buildings round. There was one evergreen tree against a fence. It was such a calm sunny day. The green grass ground was divided half and half diagonally by the shadow. A gentle breeze was playing the leaves on the tree, showing their green fronts and white backs alternately. The sun ray reflected on them, and they looked more like ladies' sequined dresses. Those brick buildings in shadow had such tender greyish mauve colour as if they were mourning. Only the mild and happy pink light of the sun illuminated all the edges to prevent me from going into too deep melancholy. There were so many sparrows on the ground. They were busy to pick up their foods, and were in dead silence. Oh, why don't they sing? Oh, why don't they play? They gave me such a pain to think that I should waste my time like this! It is all through my nuisance illness! The man began to tell me the cause of his illness. While he was working at Shepherd's Bush he caught a great pain suddenly. It was far more serious than he first thought. He was operated right up from his chest to his abdomen. He had been in this hospital more than two months and a half. Now he was going to be sent to a seaside. He was worrying so much about his wife whom he left at home.

We filled up our pipes with tobacco which I brought in, and enjoyed smoking together.

A porter came out from the hospital and ran across the garden, and went away through the back gate. The man said to me, "Ah, some poor patient must have died; you see he is gone to fetch the undertakers."

I said, "Have you noticed that porter dressed

IN THE WEST LONDON HOSPITAL

his hands with black thing like indiarubber or leather?"

"Yes, that is to prevent the poison from the dead."

In a few minutes two men came, and they all carried away a dead man covered with black cloth, on stretcher.

The man pointed to a roof, and said: "You see that little square roof. It is the skylight roof; under that roof there is the theatre. Everybody is operated there. I have finished my worst time there. But you have not done yet. The day after to-morrow you must go."

The time had come for us to go back to the ward-room. I wrote such a lot of letters and postcards to all my friends.

After the tea I had a go-round to all the patients. No. 4 had an operation the day before. He looked almost dead. He told me he had the same illness with me. I spent most time with him. We all had suppers at 6.30, and had to go to bed 7.

All the day nurses went away and a night nurse came. The curtains were dropped on each window, and all were dead silent. One electric over the nurses' table was lit. The sister was informing all day's work to the night nurse. They were whispering with such low voices. I often heard them saying, "No. 12,

A JAPANESE ARTIST IN LONDON

No. 12." That meant myself, but I could not understand what they were talking. I only saw their faces between the palm-leaves.

Sisters and nurses must be women just same with all my John Bulless friends. They were as sweet and charming as could be. But why they looked somewhat different from my other friends? I felt as if I were in a Holy Mountain, far far away from this world.

After the sister was gone, the night nurse pulled down the electric light very low, and she was eating her own supper. Now the whole room looked quite gloomy. I looked at the clock, and with some difficulty I found out its hands pointed fifteen minutes to eight.

Some time before that, Sir Beerbohm Tree gave me seats for this night, and I was intending to see his "Trilby" with one of my John Bulless friends. Alas, I got this illness. My friend had to go to the play with her friend. I began to make all sorts of mental pictures of my friends, according to the movements of the clock hands on each minute.

Ah, now they must be on the way to the theatre; now they must have arrived at the theatre. When the clock hands pointed 8.15 my heart beated so high, as it was the time that the curtain was raised up!

My eyes followed after the clock hands until

IN THE WEST LONDON HOSPITAL

11.15 P.M. Ah, the play was over! I could not sleep a few minutes longer till I finished my mental picture of my friends returning to their house.

Then I covered my face with the sheet. A few groaning voices of those poor patients sent me into a melancholy dream. The nurse so tenderly shook my pillows to wake me up. It was the next morning about five. She wanted to put a thermometer under my arm to examine my temperature.

From this day I was told to fast. Only a cup of milk, or tea, was given to me at each meal time. In the morning the attendant doctor came to see all the patients. The No. 9 was a very painful case. He must be about fifty years old. All the nurses used to call him "Dad." One day while he was steering one of those tugs on the Thames, a rope caught his left foot and it severed his foot almost off from the ankle. Only a few tendons connected it. Now the attendant doctor took off the bandages. Lo! all the skin was off. It was such a dreadful sight to look at. The two nurses got hold of his leg, and the doctor was going to wash it with some medicine. The poor man screamed and groaned so loud. Such voices! I myself felt as if I were in the Zoo rather than a human room. Poor fellow, he was such a jolly man, but he could not control himself with that terrible pain.

This day was the visiting day. After the luncheon all those families, relatives and friends of the patients, were pouring in. Here and there on the beds I saw some affectionate kisses and warm handshakes. All the poor patients, who were quite isolated from the outer world, had their hearty communication at last.

There was some indescribably cheerful atmosphere in the ward now. Those dead-pale faces had some colour. Really, this was a Ladysmith or a Mafeking day for them.

Horace Ward, one of the staffs at my publishers', came to see me. While he and I were talking, a patient was sent to the No. 2 bed, just operated a few minutes ago. He brought the full odour of ether, and he himself was so pale and quite unconscious. Ward seemed very much frightened. I told him it was a good job he did not come on the next day, or he must see me just like that!

On the next morning I was told "better to keep myself in bed," because I must be operated in the afternoon.

No. 3 was a small boy. He said he was nine, but he did not look more than five or six. He had been operated more than six times. He was no more than skin and bones. He

IN THE WEST LONDON HOSPITAL

had a large forehead, with beautiful fair hairs. His big eyes were sunken so deep. His nose and mouth were so clearly cut. Dante Rossetti might have painted such a portraiture. So I nicknamed him " Dante Rossetti's boy." This morning the nurse came to him to wash the wounds on his leg with a syringe. The poor boy knew too well that it was painful to be washed like that. But he was too weak either to cry or to move. He laid himself quite flat on the bed, and every time when the nurse poured the medicine into his wounds, he stretched his maple-leaf-like little hands and tiny, bony feet, and shivered them as if they were electrified.

Watching this poor boy from my bed I recollected my own boy life. I was such a naughty and cruel boy. I used to go around a pond in my garden and beat those little frogs with my stick. The poor frogs would stretch their four limbs straight and tremble themselves to death. Now that Dante Rossetti's boy was so much like those poor frogs I killed. So unconsciously I went into sleep for an hour or two, and I was dreaming of those poor frogs all the time.

In the afternoon the nurse told me to have a bath, and after the bath she gave me a nightshirt especially for the operation. It was too

159

A JAPANESE ARTIST IN LONDON

big for me. I could not put my hands out of its sleeves!

It was 5.10 P.M. the nurse prepared such lots of bandage in a big basket, and took me to the theatre upstairs. Dr. Baldwin was standing between a bed and all his medical instruments for my operation. He was in a white coat and white apron. I never saw him like that before. He always looked a very dignified gentleman in his frock-coat. To-day he looked exactly like a butcher. Another doctor was sitting side by him. This doctor was to put me into a magical death.

I laid down on that awfully hard and small bed.

"Doctor, you know I am such a heavy smoker, and my heart is rather weak. Do you think can I stand for a magical death?"

Dr. Baldwin put his ear to my chest.

"Your heart is quite perfect. You need not be afraid."

"I suppose the ether is not quite as bad to my heart as some charming English young ladies?"

They all laughed!

The ether operator was on my left side, and covered my nose and mouth with a large india-rubber thing.

"Now shut your eyes. Breathe in deeply

IN THE WEST LONDON HOSPITAL

from your nose, and breathe out to this tube from your mouth. Th–a–t's it! On–ce more! Th–a–t's it! On–ce more, again! Very go–o–d! Again! Th–a–t's it!"

Then suddenly he sent lots of ether at once. I wanted to say that was too much, but I could not utter a single word! While I was being treated like this, my heart was beating so high, and it sounded exactly like the steam-engine of a large boat, which you hear from your cabin.

First I saw some three dozens small red catherine wheels running round so quickly on a brown ground. Then they became less number and running slower on blue ground. Then I saw only three or four large white catherine wheels running so slowly on blue ground. At last one large light round thing jumped out from below. At the same time I threw my right hand to the other side, which somebody caught.

CHAPTER XV

IN THE WEST LONDON HOSPITAL—AFTER THE OPERATION

Where am I? Light green walls! Let me see. Ah, this must be the life class of Hopkin's Art School in San Francisco! A shadowy figure is staring at me! Who is that? Hullo, she is not quite a stranger to me. I know I saw her somewhere else before! "Oh, don't smack my face like that!"

"No. 12, can't you recognise me? I am your nurse. You are back to our ward-room now. I have brought you in."

Why! of course it was our "Accident Ward." I saw the clock hands pointing 6.10 P.M. One hour must have passed!

However fast I sleep, I can always realise about how long I have slept. But this magical death was entirely different thing to me. I did not feel there was even a few seconds in this blank one hour.

I asked the nurse, "When shall I be operated?"

IN THE WEST LONDON HOSPITAL

She said, "Your operation is finished."

No sooner than I was told "your operation is finished," I began to feel something at the operated part. First I felt a large piece of ice was fixed there. Then I felt it was a hard wooden board, and some one was striking the back of this board so hard with an iron hammer —bang, bang, bang!—as many times as my heart beated. Only a few minutes later these sounds were changed into pain! Oh, this was really painful. Who shall say toothaches are the most painful? Comparing toothaches with this pain is just same to compare Serpentine Lake with Atlantic Ocean.

The ancient Chinese poets often said, "My pain is as great as if my intestine was cut off." I realised how good expression this was.

Just the moment I was getting into my own senses the porter brought in a letter. It was from one of my Japanese friends. I had read it nearly half, then the nurses came and snatched it away, saying it was not the time for me to read any letter.

How much were my lungs saturated with the ether? On my every breath I felt the pure strong ether was coming out, and I wondered if my lungs themselves were brewing ethers.

The night was dreadful. I could not see anything in darkness, so all my nerves were

A JAPANESE ARTIST IN LONDON

concentrated to the pain. I told the night nurse that only if the electric above my bed was lit I could bear the pain much easier, but the nurse said it was the law of that hospital that all the lights should be put off in night. The tender-hearted nurse came to me so many times to soothe me down. I thought if I groaned loud it might take away a little of this pain. Shall I try it? Oh no! I am a Japanese. Peoples would say a Japanese cried in the hospital. What a disgraceful rumour might be spread out all over! So I laughed. However, the nurse knew how painful I was. She fetched the attendant doctor in and he injected my arm. It did not affect me at all. He tried twice again, only they were ineffectual every time.

The dawn came. The first bus and waggons passed by. The traffic outside the building was getting thicker. The window-curtains were raised up and the day nurses came. I began to forget my pain a great deal. But I could not move a bit yet. Warm milk was given to me in a feeding-cup. A nurse poured it down into my mouth. I think I had only warm milk or tea for about a whole week.

I had a friend to whom I used to write a letter every day. Only this day I was obliged to stop my letter-writing for whole day.

IN THE WEST LONDON HOSPITAL

The night came again, and my pain was as bad as before. A terrible sleepless night again. I was counting every minute to hear the first bus pass the building.

On the Saturday morning, after a milk breakfast, I felt so tired and began to sleep at last. I was awakened by the nurse to have a beef-tea luncheon, and I found out my pain was much subsided.

A poor man covered with all sorts of rags was brought in to No. 1. He was accompanied by his poor old wife. The wife was weeping. It must be a serious case. The man was sent to the "theatre" about six o'clock, and he was brought in on a wheeled couch to his bed again. A screen was put around the bed. A doctor and a day nurse remained inside the screen for a few minutes. I heard the wife crying.

They all came out quite soon, and I saw him through the screen. He was covered with a white sheet. It was just like that picture of George Watts' in Tate Gallery. The porter came to put him on a stretcher. All was covered with black cloth. I understood he was dead.

This night I had intervals sleep, but I was awakened by the pain so often, and I saw the nurse sometimes standing by side of my bed,

A JAPANESE ARTIST IN LONDON

and sometimes stealing herself away so quietly. Was she watching me while I was sleeping? I worshipped her back with all my heart. Tender and gentle angel was she to me!

Next day was the visiting day again. I had already many letters from my friends promising to visit me, so I was counting every minute from the morning. I believe every patient did the same with me except that "Rossetti's Boy." He was sitting up on the pillow. I saw a big crystal-like tear on his both eyes. They were getting bigger and bigger. Then his eyelids could not hold them any longer. They flowed down on his very pale cheeks, and the next tear-balls were ready on his eyes again. Every time when the tears passed over his cheeks his tiny sharp lips quivered so unconsciously. It was just like a lotus leaf with the morning dews.

Why was he so sad? On the last visiting day I saw him spoilt by his mother, who brought some toys and picture-books. Couldn't his mother come this time? I learnt from the nurse that the poor boy was told to be sent to the theatre again, so he could not be able to see his mother. I was so sorry for him!

Three P.M. at last! The entrance door was open for the visitors. Some half-dozen of my very best friends came. It was the rule of

IN THE WEST LONDON HOSPITAL

the hospital that not more than two persons were allowed to see the patients at the same time, and the visiting hour was only one hour. I was so sorry to say good-bye so soon to the first visitors, yet I wanted to see the next comers as soon as possible. I did not know what to do. They all were the quite regular visitors to me on every Sundays and Wednesdays. Among these regular visitors was Mr. Lapsley. He is the owner of a public-house called "A Bunch of Grapes" in Brompton Road. I used to go to his bar occasionally to study the English life. But certainly I could not be his profitable customer, because it was only once or twice in fortnight that I could afford myself to visit his bar. But one of those evenings he came to me and wanted to speak, as I "was the most sober customer." I wanted to buy a package of cigarettes from him. He wouldn't sell me any cigarette. He said, "Cigarette is very bad for health." He ran out of doors and came back in a few minutes. He brought me such a beautiful pipe, and offered me his own tobacco, and taught me how to bite a pipe. Ever since I have become a pipe-smoker, and I noticed that was so much better for my health.

Now, hearing that I was in the hospital, he

A JAPANESE ARTIST IN LONDON

visited on me so regularly. It was all his hearty kindness, because I myself had done nothing to him.

So many beautiful flowers were sent to me from all my friends almost every day. The nurses were delighted with them, and said they have never seen before such luxury of flowers.

About a week after my operation a little fish supper was given to me at last. This was the very first solid meal for me. On the night I had such a terrible nightmare. I dreamed all my bed-clothes were in flame, so I screamed. The nurse hurried up to me and put her hand on my forehead to see my temperature, and I was awakened. I told her about my nightmare. She said, "Oh, that was so much better. I thought you were seriously ill again. You know, No. 12, you often speak all your secrets in your dreams." I was so astonished and shy of myself. But she said, "Never mind, we nurses never repeat what the patients speak in their dreams." That made me feel easy.

But the next day I was really very poorly, and I fainted. Strange to say, that on the moment I was going to be fainted, I had exactly same mental vision as when I decided to commit suicide. I saw so plainly those portraits of my families and best friends.

IN THE WEST LONDON HOSPITAL

They thought any solid meals were too early for me, and I had to have only warm milk and tea for two days more.

As I was getting better little by little every day I began to observe everything that was going on every day. Some convalescents were sent away and new patients were brought in immediately on the same bed. That poor man on No. 9, who had the trouble with his left foot, was not getting on satisfactorily at all, and the doctors decided to amputate his leg altogether. He was sent to the theatre one morning, and when he came back to his bed and got into his conscience he groaned like a lion, and he shouted, "Oh dear, oh dear; I am damned, I am damned!"

The nurse hurried up to his side and put her hand on his mouth. But his groaning voice escaped through her fingers. Strange to say, No. 8 was an old man whose left foot was amputated at the same time. Those two old men had a race. Every morning when the attendant doctor and nurses untied their bandages, I used to watch them through the screen. It was very interesting to notice their progress. First their feet looked more like a goose ready to cook. Their flesh and skin was tied together with some cords. Gradually the skins were closing together, and then they

A JAPANESE ARTIST IN LONDON

were quite healed. They looked like an old man's bald head then. The men were sent away after that.

One midnight a patient was brought into No. 1 bed. He was a dreadful stutterer, and such a terrible deaf! The doctors and nurses used to write all that they wanted to tell him. Afterwards I learnt from a nurse that he was so deaf, that while he was walking somewhere about East Sheen, a motor came alarming its horn, but he could not hear that, so he was overrun by the motor. He had compound fracture on his both legs, and his chest had some bad injury too. On that night the porter brought in something like a big ladder, which they fixed on the back of the bed, and the doctor tied up a long tray on the patient's legs, and with many cords they were hung to that ladder. It took over two hours, and the patient was screaming all the time. I thought it was such a job for all the doctors and nurses. I sat up on my bed and watched all the process. The nurse came and said, " You naughty boy, you mustn't do that. Lay yourself down and sleep. The doctor will be very cross with you." But I was such a fox. No sooner than the nurse went away I began to sit up again. The nurse came to put me down more than once again. But Dr. Baldwin smiled at

IN THE WEST LONDON HOSPITAL

me, and said, "Are you interested with our work?"

That was such a good constitution, for the nurses never said anything when I watched that treatment next time.

Every morning after my temperature was registered, on a tablet which was hung on the wall above my bed, it was my greatest amusement to look at that list. The marks of the temperature were made twice a day, and it looked like the weather forecast of the *Daily Telegraph*.

One day a new attendant doctor came; he was very fair, and was such a gentle young fellow. He had some strong odour of chloroform. I said to him, "I suppose you are working in the theatre all day. Don't you think you might shorten your own life by inhaling the ether and chloroform every day?"

He smiled so tenderly, and shook my hand, and said, "No, Mr. Markino, you need not be afraid of that. If I go and get fresh air I shall be quite all right. It doesn't affect my life at all. Only the peoples who worry in their daily life shall surely shorten their life."

Alas, I wondered how many peoples in this world could have the natural length of their life! There are so many poor who are worrying

A JAPANESE ARTIST IN LONDON

in their daily life every day, and what this doctor said is quite true. Look at those youngsters in the poor districts, and if you ask their ages, you would be much surprised. Their faces are so worn-out; sometimes twenty-five-year-old woman looks more than forty, or even more. It is not only the poor people who have worryings; there are so many rich people who worry even more than the poor. What is the general cause of human worrying? Is there one word in which you can answer this question? Yes, there is. It is selfishness. One's selfishness is enough to make hundreds of peoples worry! Then, not only that, but there are many peoples who worry themselves all through their own selfishness. Indeed, this world is full of the disgusting odour of selfishness, and there are many poor weak-hearted victims who are made unconscious by this odour, and never come back to life again.

One morning, about sixteen days after my operation, Dr. Baldwin came to see me. I remembered his letter quite well. He had said " about two weeks or thereabout to be in the hospital." Now it was over two weeks. So I asked him how many days more should I be in the hospital. He said, " At least two weeks more." It was such a great disappointing to me. This time he has so grossly deceived

IN THE WEST LONDON HOSPITAL

me. But remembering how I did deceive him about the name of my illness, I freely forgave him, and he laughed at my idea.

I wrote to my friend how I was disheartened by this delay, and next morning I got an answer. "Where is your philosophy, then? It is not yet the time for you to count the days. What you ought to do now is to observe everything in your ward-room and write your diary, which we may publish some day." So I obeyed my friend's advice.

A constable came in his uniform. He was sent to an operation, and came back quite unconscious to No. 2 bed. He must have only a slight illness, for he got convalescent so soon. One morning a maid-servant came into our ward-room to scrub the floor. The constable was very frivolous with her, and they two made such noises. The nurse was very cross with the maid, and sent her out at once. But the nurse did not say a single word to him; and the worst thing was that the constable did not seem to be ashamed! I remember more than one of my English lady friends said to me, "If men don't behave themselves well, it is always woman's fault."

It is very, very modest of John Bullesses. But I really think men ought to control their animal passions fairly well too.

No. 6 was a middle-aged man. He must be serious, for all his families were summoned on an ordinary day—I mean not visiting day. A screen was put around the bed. I could not see him well, as his bed was the farthest one, but on the same evening the porter carried away his corpse on a wheeled stretcher and passed by my side.

A young sailor came in one day. When his operation was done, he was put in No. 5 bed. When he got into his conscience it was such an exhibition! He threw away all the bed-clothes, and stood up on his bed. The nurses put him down again and covered him with the bed-clothes, which he threw off again and again. He swung his fists all round. The cupboard was tumbled over, and the chair feet were broken. He shouted, "Don't ye know I am a boxer?"

The nurses were quite frightened. He began to call his girl's name, then he began to sing loudly all those vulgar songs. It was no more a Holy Mountain, but a regular Bank Holiday.

A doctor was sent for, and he injected morphine on the sailor's arm. That made him go quietly to sleep.

All the patients laughed at him. But I rather sympathised with him. He was a sailor

IN THE WEST LONDON HOSPITAL

—a follower of Nelson. He must have had a great pain; I know it by my own experience, only a few weeks ago. And as he was too proud to cry, so surely he acted like that to lessen his own pain! England is safe as long as she has such an innocent, childlike sailor!

June 13, Thursday. Dr. Baldwin came to examine me, and said, "You can get up." I was so happy. At 5.30 P.M. I got up and put on my Japanese kimono. Everybody was very curious of that. I felt as if a quite round ball was grown on my heel, and I had a great difficulty to keep the equilibrium to walk. I was nearly going to fall down again and again. My " Rossetti's Boy " was so anxious. " No. 12, you must go back to your bed!" I imitated purposely as if I could not walk at all, and he was so excited.

After the supper it was my great pleasure to help the nurses to wash all dishes. The next morning, soon after my temperature was taken, I got up to serve the breakfast to all the patients, and wash the dishes, then to help the night nurse to make all the patients' beds. The day nurses were surprised when they came in to see everything was already done. At luncheon and tea and supper I was a waiter as well as dish-washer. The next morning I learnt how to make beds for those serious

A JAPANESE ARTIST IN LONDON

patients. Then I helped the nurses even to do some unclean jobs.

Some patients told me, "Your hands is so soft, and your treatment is as tender as a nurse." I was awfully pleased with these flattering words. My Rossetti's Boy was very fond of me, because I used to carry him to the garden. He was as light as a newspaper. A new patient came into No. 11 bed. He was rather seriously ill, and he could not write, so I used to write what he dictated to me. All his letters were for his Missus. I have learnt a great deal about a John Bull's affection toward his Missus!

One of the nurses told me if I was a woman I could be a very good nurse. These flattering words I could not so easily accept, for there was a man on No. 8. His nature was rather greedy. The more I did to him the more he expected from me. It was only five days, but during this short time I began to get tired of him. In fact, I hated him in my heart, only I did not show my feeling to him. I thought how difficult it must be to be a nurse. I tried all the day to control myself, but I am sure that the night nurse knew that. For she often said to me, "No. 12, don't bother about the patients any more. Your breakfast is getting quite cold. Go back to your bed and eat!"

IN THE WEST LONDON HOSPITAL

I remember Mr. Spielmann told me that "great heroes are humble slaves to the public. So the King is the humblest slave of the nation after all." I must say, nurses are the greatest and noblest heroines. If all the diplomatists of a country were as humble slaves to the nation as those hospital nurses, how flourishing that country would be! If all the women were just like these nurses, I decidedly agree with the suffragettes.

But I think the noble slaves of the gentle and fairer sex should not be so rough to box the policemen or throw the stones to the window glasses!

On June 18th I had to say good-bye to all those kind sisters and nurses and those pathetic patients, and I drove a cab to Mr. Sladen's house, which was so near to the Hospital. When I came back to Sydney Street, some flowers as well as a few Japanese friends of mine were awaiting me.

CHAPTER XVI

MY HOLIDAYS IN LONDON

At the same time when I was discharged from the West London Hospital I was told by my publishers to go to Paris at once to make a book, "The Colour of Paris." I was still quite weak, and the doctors insisted that I should go to a seaside at least for a week or two. But I decided to spend my holidays in London, because I love London so much, and if I go to any country place I get homesick for London, from the second day. Once or twice I went out into the country before, but always I was miserable, and when my train came to the London suburb I always felt so happy. Perhaps the seaside air might be healthier for me, but I knew nothing could be better for my health than to feel happy, and I am so happy in London.

During this short holiday I made a very valuable acquaintance.

As I mentioned in the former chapter, Mr. Spielmann has been always the custom house

MY HOLIDAYS IN LONDON

of all my English friends. But this was the only one exception—Mr. Meinertzhagen bought a copy of "The Colour of London." He wanted to meet me. He went to some Picture Gallery to get my private address. The gallery people refused to give him my address. Only if he had gone to my publishers they would be delighted to do so, but Mr. Meinertzhagen read my essay in the book. He saw that I said I had a friend in a little newspaper shop in Chelsea. Poor Mr. Meinertzhagen walked all over Chelsea to inquire every newspaper shop. He had nearly two hours' walk, and at last he found out the one. The shopman said, "Yes, a Japanese gentleman comes to my place every day, sir, but I don't know his address. He always comes from the direction of Sydney Street."

Mr. Meinertzhagen asked a telegraph boy who was walking in Sydney Street, and so found me out.

When Confucius was asked what was the happiest thing in his life, he replied, "Friends come to seek me from the far-away distance. Could it not be the happiest thing?"

Strange to say my tailor's son, Fred, was working under Mr. Meinertzhagen at the Chelsea Conservative Club. So I often visited that Club. I don't know much about the

A JAPANESE ARTIST IN LONDON

political sects, but I was delighted to meet with those Conservative peoples because they all looked so Briton! And I felt so flattered to be called a Chelsea Conservative. This was the reason I called the first chapter of my Chelsea life "Chelsea Conservative."

While I was in Paris I had dreams and reveries of London most every day. On June 23rd, 1908, I left Paris. When I arrived at "New Heaven" once more, the first thing I noticed was a policeman in his uniform, who was standing on the wharf. My tears came out to see the real Briton again.

My publishers knew I loved Chelsea, and they engaged a room at Markham Square in Chelsea for me. I had awfully jolly time meeting with all my old Briton friends again.

But I think I was such a funny fool! Although I myself used to talk against many things in Paris, I got angry at once if my English friends talked badly against Paris. Every time when they talked in that way, I recollected all my dear French friends. How could I make double faces for them!

During this holiday I got a letter from some old Irish lady in Dublin. First of all she mentioned that she was delighted with my essay in "The Colour of London," and she said, "I am an old lady, but remember, I never show

MY HOLIDAYS IN LONDON

the linings all round my skirt on wet days, so I hope you would not be shocked at me." Then she wrote that she wanted me to do a London sketch for her. She particularly mentioned that she was not an extravagant art collector, so she could not afford to pay me a big price. "Will you let me know your usual price?"

At first I thought I could give my sketch at any price, or even as a present for such a sweet lady. Then I rethought that if that lady was a rich aristocratic lady, she might think I was insulting her.

Therefore I answered her like this. "Now I am having holidays in London, and I am making studies of London sketches. For those studies I don't mind the prices at all. If you send me £6, that will pay me quite well, but the highest price I ever got for my sketches was £20. Whether you pay me £6 or £20 my work will be exactly same, because I cannot regulate my art study according to the price."

To my delighted surprise, she sent me a cheque of £20 on the return post. Now my feeling is not about the money matter. I am sure she could not imagine how I was appreciating her generosity, and that how her generosity made me feel comfortable in my English life.

A JAPANESE ARTIST IN LONDON

It seemed to me that I was born not to be perfectly happy. For as I began to have less hard-up life, I was caught by a bad brain illness and I had to pass terrible life for some weeks. But once more I was floated on the surface of a bright life, when I was told to go to Rome with my best friends.

From October 1908 to May 1909 I was in Rome, in order to illustrate "The Colour of Rome." On June 4th I came back to London, and on the first day I had a dinner at the Imperial Restaurant of S. Kensington, Station Building. I saw on the top of the menu "Imperial Restaurant and Hotel." I knew this restaurant for some ages, but never knew it was "Hotel." I asked the manager if I could stay here, and he made a special arrangement for my room. The peoples in this restaurant are all Italians, and I made friendship with them all at once.

From the middle of September 1909 to December 1909 I was sent to Oxford to illustrate "Oxford From Within," and only lately I came back to my restaurant, which I call "Ye Olde Neste" because it is so comfortable to me. How delighted I was to enjoy myself every day in this old nest of mine again.

On Christmas Eve I walked all round the

MY HOLIDAYS IN LONDON

streets, and was so excited with Christmas shops and jolly peoples. Everywhere was so crowded and it was such a good study. My landlord gave me box of a hundred nice Egyptian cigarettes, the same ones he charges 1d. each for. I was so pleased, and at night he offered me port wine for my dinner. He is quite a darling.

I had such a jolly Christmas. The restaurant was closed all day, and all the lodgers were gone. I was only the one left. They cleared out all those small tables and made one large table. All the landlord's family and waiters and I had such a big Italian dinner at two o'clock. Then they had dances, Neapolitan songs, and all sorts of Italian games. It was just like "Est-Est-Est" or "Uomo piccolo." I had so many cups of champagne and Italian wines for luck and I was too jolly, like a pigest pig!

On New Year's Eve I went to St. Paul's. It was very different from my imagination; far, far more crowds were there. The manager of this restaurant said, "It will be too rough for you to go there alone," and he took me there at 10.30. I took a sketch book with me. But lo! it was absolutely impossible to sketch. For one hour and half we were just like sardines! More than once I thought I might

A JAPANESE ARTIST IN LONDON

be flattened like a kipper! Only the manager stretched his arms and protected me, so I could breathe.

It was a great fun and I was awfully amused, but not at all good for art. I saw some peoples peeping from those windows of the surrounding houses. I envied them very much. If I could be in one of those windows I am sure I could make a very good sketch.

About 11.15 one night, not long after the New Year's Day, I was having a little glass of brandy in the restaurant. A man came in. He was well dressed; evidently he must be a gentleman. I judged him as a sportsman. But his head was bleeding, and he was rather too jolly. The manager was frightened. The man was repeating same thing over again and again, saying he had been knocked by a taxi-cab, but he did not like to accuse the driver.

At first I did not take any notice. He ordered some whisky, and was talking with the waiters. Then he turned his face to me and said, "You are Japanese?"

I only nodded my head.

He said he knew the Japanese Military Attaché in Paris.

I only nodded my head again. I was rather frightened to get trouble with "too jolly" people.

MY HOLIDAYS IN LONDON

Then he said :

"Do you know a very well-known Japanese artist called Yoshio Markino?"

I only smiled.

Then he said, "Ah, you have a splendid brother; you must be proud of him. You know, I always admire his works very much, and he writes most interesting thing. Last time he published 'The Colour of Rome' with Miss Olave Potter. O, such a splendid book! I bought three copies—one for myself, and two for two of my lady friends as Christmas presents."

I walked to his table and took out my card-case and put my card on his table, and came back to my table again.

He was so surprised. Although he was so drunken he tried to be as serious as he could, and expressed his delight. He said, "You may don't believe me, because you know . . . I am not . . . quite ri' to-night. But believe me, I am a grea' 'mirer of that book."

Then he said, "Didn't you shay Markino an Facchino, an you pre-fered Newcasshle-'n-Tyne, an tha' English morals ish beautiful box well-locked?"

O, he remembered everything quite well. So I began to trust him, and talked to him.

It was one of these idle evenings I went to

A JAPANESE ARTIST IN LONDON

the Empire Theatre to see the Ballet which my friend Mr. Wilhelm had arranged. Before the ballet I saw a man who imitated many well-known peoples. At the end he gave an imitation of King Edward. All the auditors so gracefully stood up and paid their homage. It struck my feelings very much indeed. It was neither the King himself nor his real portrait; it was only a music-hall artist. But for his imitation, all the British auditors paid all their homage! I remember when I was in Japan some seventeen years ago, those ignorant American missionaries were so foolishly preaching that "the real Christian" should not worship any person—even the Emperor. There was one Japanese (only one among 45,000,000 population!) who was foolish enough to take the missionaries' word so seriously and refuse to bow down before our Emperor's portrait. All the newspapers discussed him very much. I don't know how the Japanese Christians are getting on nowadays, as I have never gone back to my country since then. But if the foreign missionaries must be sent to Japan, I sincerely hope they should be from those refined Britons who worship even the imitation of the King.

Just lately I passed the under-passage from the S. Kensington Museum to the District

MY HOLIDAYS IN LONDON

Railway station. The passage is curved at the bottom. There is an illuminated lettering, "To the Railway Station. Keep to the Right." And moreover, there is an index, pointing to the Right, as if only the lettering alone were not enough. Why, there is no other way! One who comes to this way is obliged to go to the right. Then, what for is this? This is awfully Briton and I love it.

I am at present enjoying the London fogs ever so much, especially after missing two London winters.

Lately my Japanese friend opened a Japanese shop just near my place, and he is a frequent visitor. We have talks together as I used to have with my other Japanese friends some three years ago. One day he said to me, "Whatever is your idea and wherever have you got it? Certainly it is not Japanese idea, and if not English either, what shall I call it? Pray don't call your book 'Japanese Impressions,' or else the public may be puzzled."

I answered him, "Amen! I myself don't know what I am now!"

CHAPTER XVII

CONCLUDING CHAPTER

AFTER being away for three times, how did that effect upon my impression of London? It is true that I loved the *très chic* colour in Paris; it is true that I loved the gay sunshine in Rome; and it is true that I loved those old gothics in Oxford. But after some absences from London I began to love London even more than before.

It was just five days after I came back from Rome that I was invited to a dinner at the Parliament by one of my M.P. friends. When I arrived at Westminster station I was about a few minutes too soon to go in, so I had a little walk on the Embankment. It was still daylight. I saw St. Thomas's Hospital across the Thames. My head was still full of those old ruins in Rome, and those delicate colours of Parisian buildings, and I said to myself, " How ugly colours are those London buildings! "

The dinner was finished at 9.30, and we all went out to the Terrace to have a walk. London was in her most beautiful evening

CONCLUDING CHAPTER

dress. I repented that I said St. Thomas's was ugly just a few hours ago. The rows of those Hospital Buildings were silhouetted up and down against the soft, misty sky; Westminster Bridge, just like many rainbows high up, connected that distance with the foreground. All of them were in bluish (perhaps a little greenish) grey. Pale electric lights, and the warm umber lights of 'buses on the Bridge, were reflected on the full tide. A few tugs were guided by small steamboats. These were all in one tone of greyish mist. In the foreground, the pavement of the Terrace, many semicircles were marked under many a lamp. Ladies in white, and gentlemen's white chests, broke the darkness here and there. They were walking together as light as butterflies. Where else could such romantic view be seen? Neither in Paris nor Rome, I am sure!

Perhaps the real colours of some buildings in London might be rather crude. But this crude colour is so fascinating in the mists. For instance, that house in front of my window is painted in black and yellow. When I came here last summer I laughed at its ugly colour. But now the winter fogs cover it, and the harmony of its colour is most wonderful, and I am sure I need a great deal of study to paint this beautiful colour. When I was in

Rome I often exclaimed, "Only if Rome had London fogs!" Paris often had fogs, but her colour is quite soft enough on the clear days, so any little fog made Paris colour rather weak, and not so lovable as London.

Then about the life of London, I have found out it is larger than any other town. London is on the extremely larger scale altogether. She is just like a vast ocean where sardines as well as whales are living together. If a millionaire of other towns comes to London, he could not be proud of his own wealth. If a beggar comes to London, he would be surprised to see some one poorer than he. A most beautiful stranger could not expect to be crowned for her beauty, and an ugly foreigner need not be ashamed of his ugliness. Wise and fool both shall not be put to the extreme ends either. Perhaps even the robbers and pickpockets may find enough friends!

London contains more variety of life than anywhere else. I myself always find out some friends with equal height. I mean, same degree of head and heart and pocket too. Nothing could be more comfortable than to meet with friends of the same degree in everything. This is the great reason I feel so homely in London more than any other place. Then, also, it is my pleasure to share sympathy

CONCLUDING CHAPTER

with the peoples inferior to me, and to respect the peoples superior than myself. Now and then at teas, at dinners, or at clubs, I often see a glimpse of some wonderful persons. I feel as if I am diving in a mysterious ocean and see the fins and tails of some monstrous fishes. It is my ambition to discover their whole figures some day when I get a chance. Then, let me classify all John Bulls and John Bullesses as Linnæus, or Grey did the botany!

I so often meet with the English peoples who express their mad admiration of Japan. Of course there are several who really understand everything Japanese, but in a greater majority they make me quite disappointed. May I call those peoples curio-lovers? They love Japan because anything Japanese is strange to their eyes. I am much afraid these peoples shall get tired of Japan sooner or later.

I am in mad love of London, but it is not at all my curiosity. I have been here long enough. Once I loved London for curiosity: once I was rather homesick. But those periods in my life have passed away a long time ago. Now I love London because I have found out the real art and real comfort in her. London life suits me so well. Of course I love my country best, and I do not want my

A JAPANESE ARTIST IN LONDON

country too much Europeanised; "Japan ought to be Japan for ever" is my sincere desire.

Therefore I think such a person like me, who is in mad love of England, must stay in England. My own intention is to pass my life among the pure Britons and find out more Art in them.

Perhaps I love humans more than even the mists. Let them be either good or bad, I cannot live without them. I hear that artists or writers generally seclude themselves in a lonely place to find out some idea to work out. I am quite reverse. Whenever I want to get idea for painting or writing, I always throw myself amongst the thickest crowds such as Earl's Court, Shepherd's Bush, or the music stands in the Parks. Let the crowds push me to and fro—I call it a human bath. In this human bath I always work out my ideas. And if I am left quite alone, I feel too miserable to do anything.

When I was in Oxford I had no friend, and I often thought I might become a madman. I am so lucky to say I have made so many English friends—up from the Cabinet ministers down to a boot-repairer—and I love them all so dearly. Only there is one thing I am very cautious about. That is, I am always trying very hard to avoid any business matters with

CONCLUDING CHAPTER

my English friends. They all are very nice to me. But no sooner than I have to do any business with them, I ever so often have been disappointed with them. Oh, how often have I sunken into delusions! It has been my question for a long time. Only very lately I have discovered something about it. I think I am not mistaken, so let me write it out now.

In Japan we have some unwritten law and invisible spirit which has been overruling all Samurais. This is called Bushido, and sometimes called Yamato Damashi, or the Soul of Old Japan. In England there is an unwritten law and invisible spirit too—I must call it "The Soul of England." The Soul of Old Japan is Honour, and the soul of England is Business. For the sake of Honour many Samurais had dead-heat duels with their dearest friends, and for the sake of Honour the fathers often stabbed their children unto death. In England Business has the power almost the same with Honour in Japan. I often notice my English friends change their expression and knock the table with their fists and say, "Ah, but this is the Business." For "business" laughter gets serious, drunkards get sober, friends quarrel, and lovers depart each other. English husbands would bring their wives to the court, all for the business matter.

A JAPANESE ARTIST IN LONDON

Of course I know that English peoples do much for Honour also, but in Japan it is only the merchants who do the business, while in England it may even be that Princes have business.

If this business soul is used properly it is just as graceful as the soul of Honour. They both ought to come to the same finishing point—that is to say, one who esteems Honour shall have business fair, and the best business men shall esteem Honour. I think this is the great reason why England is the head of her commonwealth in this world. But if both the soul of Japan and the soul of England were misdirected, they both would be as ugly as possible. The former would be too quick-tempered, while the latter would be too mean. They both are just like some drugs. If you take them in proper way you will save your life from death, and if you take them in wrong way you shall poison yourself unto death. But how many peoples could be always in right way? We must remember we all human beings could not always be perfect. Therefore we must forgive each other's faults. And as I am a Japanese I have a natural tendency to get into my own fault and throw away friendship for the sake of Honour. Frankly, I cannot bear if one thinks of a few shillings more than a warm-hearted friendship.

When the soul of Business is misled by some

CONCLUDING CHAPTER

inferior human, it is beyond what I can bear. These sorts of people often think that they can easily take advantage of me, because I am "soft." How greatly they are mistaken of me! It is only my etiquette not to struggle a little money matter with them in fear that it would injure our noble humanity. But am I afraid of any people? Never. Even if this whole world become my enemy, I cannot feel any fear. What shall I do with those peoples who act some mean thing upon me? There is one word, "Adieu for ever." Because I cannot have friendly feeling with them any longer. Everything is finished with them. What should I do throwing away all my friends like this? That is why I said the best way is not to have any business matter with my English friends. If your cat steals your fish, it is not the fault of your cat, but the fault of your own self, and you can love your cat well if you are cautious enough!

As long as no business is concerned, they all are perfectly darlings!

However, I am so lucky to say I have a few friends who are as fair in business as their own faces. To me they are just like three or five bright stars on the western evening sky. As the night is getting darker they become brighter and brighter, and shine on the dark path for

A JAPANESE ARTIST IN LONDON

me to march on. With these friends I can share my sorrow as well as my joy in the business matters.

Are these few peoples only the bright stars in whole London? or are there many as fair as these friends? I don't know that, and I don't want to know either. Friendship is by quality and not by quantity. These are enough for me to feel it is worth of me living!

Now let me have a few words about my art. Although it is some seventeen years since I left Japan, most time I have wasted for my living. So my study on art was not much. It was not more than twelve months that I attended at the art school in San Francisco, then about two years in London Art Schools, which were only two hours in each night. When I removed to Chelsea I began to study the London views; I wasted much time owing to the lack of materials—sometimes I had no paper to work on.

It is only since I started to illustrate the "Colour of London" that I so luckily have been able to devote all my time entirely to study, and this is the third year. Therefore I must say my study of art is only six or seven years all together. Though I am growing older and older every day with the same rate with all the readers, my art is only seven-year-old

CONCLUDING CHAPTER

child! I know it is about ten years behind. I often feel very sad about it, but it is altogether too foolish to lament about the past, which shall never come back. Only I shall try to take care of my health to prolong my life, and shall patiently expect my success some day in future. I am in the same idea with that Japanese philosopher who made a poetry of six "no's"—" I have no parents, no wife, no children, no home, and though I have no money, I have no idea to die yet."

Since some of my works appeared in the form of two or three books, some critics as well as my intimate friends have given me most flattering advices in papers or by letter. I am very thankful to all. Only one thing I must beg sincerely to all my kind sympathisers: "Pray do not take me as quite an artist yet." If you look upon seven-year-old art as a master, whatever shall become of this world? Some talked about "Japanese Art or European Art?" About this question I have a few words to say.

Yes, Japan has her own Art. The scholars have to learn how to hold the brush and how to draw lines. These practices are just like that of violinists. It would take some ten or fifteen years before they can paint any of their own compositions. Some of them follow

A JAPANESE ARTIST IN LONDON

very faithfully after their master, and some are founding their own schools. You can call them all "Japanese styles." How those old Japanese masters would lament if they knew peoples were calling anything new or different "a Japanese style"! Now the reader can clearly see I do not belong to any Japanese style. It is true that I have studied charcoal drawings at some schools, but it was only my study to get the shape from the nature, and I was far below following any European styles. Then all the rest of my study has been entirely myself-taught. Then, why am I European style? It is true that I have learned such sciences as perspective or anatomy through books. You may call them "European sciences," but I learnt them, not because they were European, but because I found them so true to Nature. Is anything quite natural called "European"? I think it is a very narrow-minded logic. Not only Europeans alone, but Japanese, Chinese, Indians, and Negroes shall come to the same point if they are faithful to Nature.

Another question reached to me, "Why don't you paint more differently from us, because you are a Japanese?"

A more laughable remark was, "You will lose your art unless you stick to the Japanese style."

CONCLUDING CHAPTER

To these peoples I sincerely ask, What is the definition of the word "Art"? Perhaps they may say, "Art is something different from ordinary things." They might be pleased if I painted English women with one eye or three eyes, or if I painted London Bridge on the top of St. Paul. They would say, "Ah, this is charming Japanese Art because it is so uncommon!"

But how could I do such things? I can see the beauty of English women as well as the English peoples do, and I can unfortunately, or rather, fortunately, see the beauty of London as exactly she is now. If I paint English women not really so beautiful as they really are (very sadly I always cannot paint so), that is my own fault, and not my Art by any means.

My definition of the word "Art" is "Well selected," and I faithfully obey to my own definition. I could not be such a speculator to distinguish myself with anything only different.

At present, I am in mad love of London seen quite naturally, and I cannot pretend myself to make any style or mannerism which would only mean a handicap to my study. All the books I am making now are only my studies. Only if I were rich enough to get daily bread without selling my pictures I should never show such studies to the public. This is quite understood by my publishers. But some day I shall be something more than a slave of nature. That is to say, I shall establish my own school. Here I shall keep myself silent and let my brush speak it in the future when I am ready. At present I am contented to be " one of many."

When I finished writing this book I showed it to some friends : they looked rather amazed because I have written about my friends and everything " too directly," and I have come back to my own conscience to think that I might have written too much. But I am not clever enough to conceal the fact and I am not hypocrite enough to tell a lie. So this book itself is I myself. When Confucius made Shunju, he said, " It is this book through which the public will know me. It is this book through which the public will condemn me." I must say, too, that it is this book through which I may get bitter enemy. It is this book through which I may get real friends. Anyhow, it is this book through which the public will know me thoroughly.